W9-BWI-889

STIR, CHANGE, CREATE

STIR, CHANGE, CREATE

by

KENNETH L. PIKE

WILLIAM B. EERDMANS PUBLISHING COMPANY
GRAND RAPIDS, MICHIGAN

acknowledgments

The author gratefully acknowledges the assistance of the following colleagues in the preparation of this book: Bud Larsen, for illustrations and drawings; William E. Speedy, for basic layout and design; Ethel Wallis, assisted by Carolyn Muller, for the editing of the manuscript; Eunice Pike, for the editing of chapel talks used as essays.

The author wishes to thank the editors and publishers of the following journals for permission to reprint material which appeared in their publications:

His (official organ of the Inter-Varsity Christian Fellowship): "Left-Handed" (June, 1962); "Pseudo-Immortality" (January, 1968).

Moody Press and Moody Bible Institute: **Not Alone,** by Eunice V. Pike, pp. 52-58.

Sudan Interior Mission: the essay "Breakthrough," by Mr. Harold Fuller, from **Africa Now,** number 31.

The Church Herald: "God in History" (Jan. 14, 1966); "Tempted to Quit" (July 15, 1966); "The Disillusioned Scholar" (September 9, 1966).

William B. Eerdmans: the poem "Pride" in **With Heart and Mind,** by Kenneth L. Pike.

Wycliffe Bible Translators: the poem "Crushed," **Translation,** Fall, 1965; Chapter 11, "Pike Persuaded," **Two Thousand Tongues to Go** (Harper and Row).

contents

... what's on my mind (a preview)

I am a scholar. The greatest proportion of my time is devoted to scholarship.

I am a Christian. I am devoted to Christ, risen from the dead, my Lord.

Is it strange to hybridize these two roles of mine? Let me give my first commercial:

> The Word of God needs to be translated for the little tribes all around the world. **I believe that it is especially appropriate that scholars be involved in Bible translation.**

If you are interested in studying **how** to analyze a language that has no alphabet or dictionary, write to the Summer Institute of Linguistics, Inc., Box 1960, Santa Ana, California 92702. If you want information regarding results, write the Wycliffe Bible Translators, Inc., Box 1960, Santa Ana, California 92702.

Few of us remember that a large proportion of the pages of the Bible were written by the equivalent of Ph.D.'s. Daniel was on the level of a Ph.D., not a fuzzy-cheeked boy. He was under competitive examinations at the top of his culture in Israel, and enrolled in a graduate area study program ("skillful in all wisdom, and cunning in knowledge, and understanding science — whom they might teach the learning and the tongue of the Chaldeans," Daniel 1:4). When he presented his competitive doctoral dissertation, the king was honorary chairman of his committee.

Moses was more than a Ph.D. Not only did he know all the wisdom of Egyptian engineering, but also all its hieroglyphics; he was a powerful orator (Acts 7:22). God broke his proud spirit and led him back to be identified with his people and to give us a large part of the Bible.

But the scholars who wrote the Bible were also involved in social action.

There is a rigid demand in the Word of God for a social order; and God in the Old Testament made rejection of social justice one of the bases for the rejection of the people of God.

Our ancestors looked at the individual; we must now also look at society. Christ made the generalization that the poor would be with us always (Matthew 26:11). We may have the mistaken idea that we can get rid of poverty by medicine or other means, as is being attempted in India. But this allows more people to live — and the poor remain.

There is a priority that an ethic of fairness and rugged individualism has to be careful of, lest it try to send rain only on the just. God sent His rain on the unjust as well. The sun rises on all, and the rain falls on all. If we allow our goodness to be applied only to someone who is good, then we refuse to apply goodness to someone who is bad. We reply with harsh words to someone who gives us harsh words, and eventually there is an automatic demand for evil to reply with evil. My actions at that point are not determined by my character but by the character of evil, and only good social action stimulates a good action from me. In the face of evil, then, can I be good? "Be ye therefore perfect, even as your Father in heaven is perfect" — whose social action gives rain upon the just and the unjust. Do not let evil control us, but let us control evil with good.

But where does a new social order come from, one producing social good? The answer is that in the plan of God a new social order sometimes has been initiated not by society as a whole, but by an individual within that society. Abraham was called out of Ur of the Chaldees, from a corrupt social order, and God promised that from him all society would be blessed. Abraham as an individual was the father of many nations, and as an heir to his faith, I am his child — socially.

And is there, then, a mother? The Bible says there is. In the book of Galatians we read about the Jerusalem which "is from above," which is the "mother of us all." Our own children are brought up in the womb of a culture, in the matrix of society. (Although Calvin would have called the

Church, rather than a culture, our mother — see Book IV, Chapter I, of his **Institutes**.) Whether I like it or not, my children in school are affected by the cultural climate. We have to keep our schools clean if we want a good chance of keeping our children clean.

The individual in culture is man, in the image of God, a citizen of heaven. What is it that man shares with God? Not fingernails, not hair, not eyebrows. Of course, the capacity for love and for joy — but these abstracts are very hard to study through science. There is one special thing, accessible to science, that we share with God. In the beginning was the **Word.** In the beginning was **One who could talk** — not a dynamo, not brute power, not some vague pantheistic all in all, but One who could talk to Himself in the Trinity, Father to Son, and Son to the Father. This ability to communicate, to think, to reason, to plan, is ours by the creative capacity of God. Not only can we mimic it, but we ourselves become creative.

Language is in the creative image of God.

This is an intended metaphor — not accidental — at the heart of the Bible. It is at the heart of the universe, and at the heart of personality. Without language you could not say, "I ought," or "I will." Nor could you say, "You must." Personality, in part, comes from language. Language expresses character. Jesus said, "I am the light of the world." He also said, "I am the truth." He, in person, is the truth, and He said of the Father, "Thy Word is truth," and "I have given them Thy Word."

Truth comes from the person first, and Christ is at the heart of all. I am not a Platonist who looks for ultimate reality in ideas floating around in the abstract. I am a Christian who believes that Christ is the embodiment of truth, and that His words are therefore truth. Propositional revelation is true because it comes from a person who is true.

Another commercial:

> Christ prayed to the Father, "I have given them
> Thy Word. . . . So send I **them** — to give the Word."
> . . . so **I am a Bible translator.**

If language is reflecting deeply the image of God, don't expect it to be simple, now or ever — nor for any theory to exhaust it. God could have made any animal, or any kind of

11

a man He chose to make. But man as we know him, and as God wanted him to be, couldn't have been shaped like an elephant, have burrowed like a worm, been constrained by the mental limits of a bird or the communication restrictions of a moth. So it is with the incarnation of the message of God in the nature of Jesus Christ. Don't expect it to be simple. Language is complicated, because language has its source in **person**.

Language identifies person. When God named Himself "I Am," He used language to identify the self-consciousness that can talk, since "in the beginning was the Word." Language identifies us. "Surely thou art also one of them — thy speech betrayeth thee." When the Ephraimites came to the ford of the Jordan they said "sibboleth" instead of saying "shibboleth" because they couldn't form the right groove in the blade of their tongue. Delete: 42,000 Ephraimites.

Next commercial:

They needed a practical course in phonetics!

Language is an identificational factor. In John 10:4 we read that the sheep hear His voice, and they follow Him. No other voice will they follow. The dead in the grave will hear the voice of the Son of God, and they will rise.

Life is deeper than language, and life is deeper than the intellect that works through language. Faith does not begin where logic leaves off. One of the most serious errors in our student world is the notion that logic precedes faith. But faith always, inevitably, and without exception must precede logic, intellect, judgment, and reason (and then it must go beyond them). Why? Logicians and mathematicians sometimes discuss the basis for our formal intellectual processes. A logician can't begin until he adopts without proof (but by faith) some pre-logical notions; he then prepares a set of axioms either with faith in their truth or arbitrarily for an abstract meaningless system. Faith does not begin where logic leaves off: faith precedes logic. The intellect operates only within the matrix of faith, and by faith goes on beyond the limits of its insights. And "he that cometh to God must believe that **He is**" (Hebrews 11:6). He who wants to be rational must first believe.

No wonder therefore that Christ said (Matthew 18:3): Except you humble yourself as a little child, you cannot enter

12

the kingdom of God. Why did He pray (Luke 10:21): "Father, I thank you, Lord of heaven and earth, that you have hidden these things from the wise and prudent, and have revealed them unto babes. Even so, Father, for it seemed **good**. . . . " Why was it good? It is good, because a child feels simultaneously with all things coming to him at once. The logical phase of adult intellect is limited to dealing with things in a rational, articulate, formal sense, one thing at a time. Words come out of our mouths one after another. The logician and the intellectual are limited by the nature of language and the academic rational process, one thing after another.

But life cannot operate by first building a head, and then a heart, and then a toe. The embryo has to grow them, mixed all up at once, and then differentiate them. A child learning a language reacts in a similar fashion. He doesn't memorize first the verbs, then the nouns, then the syntax. He learns all at once, in a matrix, or a network. It is simultaneous integration.

It is interesting to pretend that there are two computers inside us. The first is life's integrating computer which is not articulate. It can't talk. It has groanings which cannot be uttered, because they cannot get into words. Why not? Because the elements are all together at once, coming from every direction in experience and mental storage. I hear what you are saying, I feel my emotions, and my glands circulate — all of this at once. Whatever I do with all of this afterward comes out of my mouth, through my "rational computer," one word at a time.

God's computers are not our computers. His ways are not our ways. God can do it all at once and be rational, too. But I can't be rational except by being articulate. This is far less competent than the child. All of us as linguists know this. All of us hurt when after 25 years of age we try to learn a language that requires the use of our first computers, which are stuck in a groove — and the child of six passes us by. Why? Because the life computer is an integrating computer, and the scholarly computer is a linear computer. Only as we become as children is it possible for us to have the mind of Christ and accept by faith the complexity of life, all at once, without understanding where it comes from, where it goes. Only then can we live as children with a new citizenship in heaven. Only then can we find God.

Language concentrates life's memories, truths and joys. It expresses them, and guides them, and concentrates them.

Language is a verbal telescope. We can see the galaxies in the pupil of the eye — but that pupil is only an eighth of an inch or so across. If I want to see a great distance, the image from inches of a telescope must be concentrated on the tiny surface of the pupil of my eye. A drama in two and a half hours can stir us to understand and experience something of life that we cannot see by just living, for life is too long. It is not concentrated enough. It's like the galaxy two billion light years away.

Words are like that telescope — they concentrate truth and joys. Words can concentrate revelation, and the Bible is a book of revelation. Some of the problems in the book of Genesis are nothing more than this, in my opinion. God, in order to get us to hear, had to concentrate words, as if in a verbal telescope. Although the stars look through a telescope as though one could reach out and touch them, it may take a little longer to get there in a space ship than one would think.

Language also directs and guides. The tongue is a rudder. With words we give thanks to God. If we cease to give thanks, we cease to believe. From Romans 1:21 we are led to understand that the intellectual who refused to bend his tongue to say "thank you" first, lost an essential axiom. Thinking himself wise, he became a fool. He lost the axiom that says that the fear of the Lord is the beginning of wisdom.

It is not enough to live a Christian life: there must also be **words** used. Life is not enough of a witness. Social relevance, personal integrity, personal joy, and belief must be expressed in words.

And a final commercial:

> These words of Christian witness need to be in **the vernacular.**

A Welshman once said to me, when I asked him about his mother tongue, "A man who loses his own language loses his **soul**." (He was a principal of a Baptist seminary, and I assume he was speaking in metaphorical terms!)

Some years ago I was talking with one of the greatest linguists that Denmark has produced. I said, "Why doesn't your country drop Danish and just use English — since you are teaching it nine years in your schools?" He drew himself up to his full tall height and said, "It's a good thing you asked a **friend** that question!"

Then I said to him, "Look, I'm not trying to be crude. I have given twenty-five years of my life to minority language groups, and some people say it is ridiculous. I've got to know why I'm right. Why **am** I right? Why haven't I wasted twenty-five years? You are a sophisticated, educated man and a member of a small language group. Tell me why."

He was speechless for a few moments (his initial reaction was in his integrating computer — and it took a while to bring it up to the conscious computer). Finally he said, in perfect English, "Well, you know, Pike, you lose your language and you've lost your moral substance. You've learned this at your mother's knee through stories in your own language, and it's — **you.**"

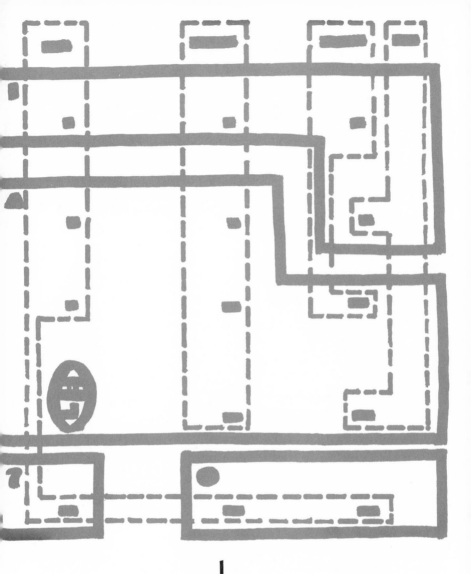

I

THE SCHOLAR
AS AN INDIVIDUAL

ME

Not other — pale imitation
Whose pseudo strength
Hides secret weakness.

Myself, for good or ill.
Ill, too much — home grown;
Good, sparse — borrowed Hence.

God wills joy;
Weal from woe —
Once weakness yields.

The Cry Is for Identity

It appears to me extraordinary that individual achievement
in one direction may be obtained only at the expense of some
deeply held desire in another direction. Our gains in social
interaction have led to a reaction in which one feels some
identity, but also alienation. We feel alienation from the very
world of society which its predecessors worked so hard to
achieve. Their goals, which at the time seemed far out,
unrealistic, idealistic, now seem commonplace.

Somehow the continual cry is for our own identity. We
want to be ourselves. I share this cry; it goes deep. I do not
want to fill an organization-man slot in a society requiring
complete conformity. But neither do I want to participate
in a rebellion which alienates me from the society without
which I have no role structure. Without role structure I have
no identity.

I become myself in fullest identity and realization by
a three-way route: first, by integration with the highest levels
of reality, reality which is personal, not irrational, not mystically
vague, not a pantheistic wholeness, but 'solid' personality.
This reality was articulated by the One from Nazareth who
said, "I am the life" (John 14:6) and reflected His internal
source with the Father who earlier had given His name as
"I AM THAT I AM" (Exodus 3:14).

19

Secondly, this identity comes in relation to the society which I try to serve. It is a relation to a society which teaches me, socializes me, gives me certain ideals and goals.

Thirdly, the identity comes by my action as an individual. The right to rebel is still within me. I can rebel against God — which is my right as an individual — but with enormous loss, because I tear myself by the roots from the very source of power without which I cannot wholly be myself. I can rebel against society, I can attempt to destroy it, but the penalty is to destroy the structure without which I cannot be myself, since only within it can some of my identifying roles be exercised. Or I can even rebel against myself as an individual, with pistol to grey matter.

I want to be me; not someone else; not buried in a mere mass; not simply conformed to other structures forced upon me. I want to be me in the deepest sense possible for an individual. As Jesus said, "You shall love the Lord your God first, and your neighbor **as yourself**." Unselfishness does not require me to hate myself, nor to ignore my best interests in this life and the one to come. Rather it places the rights, needs, and wishes of others **on a par** with my own. ("Mommy, can I have a cookie — and can Billie have one too?")

Here, then, is a three-way commitment: integration with the God of eternity, the God of individuality, the God of personal characteristics, the God who can say, "I am"; commitment to society and service to God without which I cannot have a role or be myself; commitment to the deepest aspirations of myself — excepting the right to rebel. I refuse this right, that by positive choice I may integrate with myself, with the world, and with God.

I want to be an individual. So do others.

God and the Individual

As I meet my academic colleagues around the country the first or second thing they are likely to bring up against the exclusivism of Christianity is the fact that it represents a small minority of people. We are in the minority, and this seems outrageous to the intellect. I grant it, and I have no good defense of it intellectually (although proponents of a new scientific theory do not want it rejected by majority vote). But I see some curious analogues.

Take the matter of Sir Alexander Fleming who was looking at some kind of gelatin with a smear of deadly culture on it. He noticed in the middle of it a spot where the growing culture was killed, and somehow that little growing circle caught his attention. He realized that on that gelatin base was a deadly enemy of a deadly disease.

Now for a man to see healing for the world in a spot a few millimeters wide took insight. Anybody with a statistical mind could well have said, "A quarter of an inch to save a quarter of a million people? That's ridiculous." But Fleming didn't think so.

Ideally, scientists try to find one cell, and suck it up into a little pipette just wide enough for that cell. They have just enough nutrient in that little glass tube to nourish it. They let it grow there in sterile environment so that nothing else will kill it (for it may be strong enough to kill one particular disease, but fragile enough to be killed by another). Finally it grows out of its confining tube into the nutrient around it. Then it is ready to be put into a bigger test tube. Maybe it gets contaminated, so they take a little bit out by itself and let it start over again. Finally they get it clean in the test tube, then in a bottle, then in a large vat — and presently there is penicillin for the healing of the world.

God, I read, worked with man in an analogous way. He picked out a cell, and put it in a pipette surrounded with nutrient; this was Noah, with his family. The family grew, and became contaminated. Then God reached down again and picked out one cell, Abraham, the father of us all as far as faith is concerned. God put this one man and his family in a test tube in Palestine, and let them grow to be a group of 70 people. Then He took them down into the big vat of Egypt, the cultural tub where they grew into a much larger group. He separated them from their surroundings by making them slaves, so they wouldn't so easily get contaminated by their environment. Then He moved them back to Palestine where they could grow and develop a culture which understood the vocabulary of sacrifice, and where they could be given laws to demand righteousness.

Again they went sour. God picked up a part of them and moved them into captivity where again some of them went sour and disintegrated. God picked up small groups including Zerubbabel, and later Nehemiah. He brought them back once more into Palestine and once more let them grow. And again they went sour. But in the meantime they had learned certain things. They had learned the language of blood sacrifice. They had learned the language of the individual who is known by God: "I am the God of Abraham, of Isaac, and of Jacob," and made a claim utterly different from other claims of the Orient. He was saying, "I am the God of the individual, the God who knows you **by name**."

Another analogue supports this lesson. Consider the development of hybrid corn. Pfister inbred tassel with ear, and grew nubbins. He inbred again, and got a little crop. The heat came, and the drought, and he "let the weaklings die." He inbred again, and planted again, and the weaklings died when the bugs came in to eat them. Finally he crossbred a few little nubbins which had survived drought and heat and bugs.

He was breeding into a few nubbins the concentration of certain desired genetic characteristics, throwbacks of many hundreds of generations of corn. They would not feed many people, but he built into them resistance against bugs and disease. In due time, by crossbreeding the nubbins, the result was food for the world, doubling the corn crop in many places.

This, I believe, is a picture of what God is doing with the individual. He takes Abraham out from the city and leaves the mass. He builds into him spiritual principles. He teaches him to respond to a personal God, the God of Abraham, and also the God of history, the God who moves in events.

God works with individuals, one at a time, to turn them into "penicillin," or "food" for the world. Mere numbers won't do the job; their contaminated character can kill the patients. Nor can size serve alone — nor power and prominence.

THE LEAST
SHALL BE GREATEST

Saul, big man,
   From least of tribes;

David, little man,
   Sheep of greatest flock.

The man himself —
   Not his source.

God sees
   And values heart.

I Samuel 9:21; 13:14; 16:11-12

Values —

our crucial ill, and shame.
Somehow a magnificent star may excite more wonder than the
seed-principle in a virus.

What makes for worth? Size?
Was Saul greater than David?
Power?
Was Hitler greater than the meekness of
Nazareth?
Which has greater value, dominance or service?
The Man from Nazareth made this clear: The least may
be greater. Character of heart provides the yardstick.
The scholar has no monopoly on Heart. It is found in the
deepest jungle, it roams on the plains of the herder.
Would to God that Heart were wedded to Mind.

Matthew 20:25-28

25

What makes for worth? Conformity? A curious dilemma tears us apart. On the one hand, we value our independence and individuality. On the other hand, we long to fit, to belong, to merge into the crowd inconspicuously, to be like everyone else. If we are "different," we hurt. We may resent being dressed in clothing different from our peers — or may resent being left-handed. An analogous problem faces us in the spiritual realm. Somehow, for peace to be with us, we must reconcile the two — accept differences, welcome them as evidences of individuality, use them as sources of integrating with the community as specialized members serving it.

LEFT-HANDED

Are you spiritually left-handed? Do you have a way of witnessing that you consider valid but that doesn't match the technique of your neighbors? Is strength in your left arm instead of your right, where it "ought to be"?

Then you are a "left-handed" Christian. Left-handers had a special place in Old Testament times. These men were unusual, and their differentness was the key to their usefulness. Here are three examples.

At one time, 26,000 fighting men from the tribe of Benjamin were gathered together (Judges 20:16). Seven hundred of them were specialists: they "could sling stones at a hair's breadth, and not miss." But everybody considered them odd, or perhaps special. They were left-handed.

Why were right-handers not included? One reason might be that people who lived on a hill in those days sometimes cut the path going to their city so that it spiralled upward clockwise around the hill. This put the average man attacking them at a disadvantage. A right-handed man climbing the ramp couldn't move along close to the hill side of the path and still lob stones over the wall above. So the attacking force would choose a squad of left-handed men for the lead troops.

This essay reprinted by permission of HIS, student magazine of Inter-Varsity Christian Fellowship, © 1962.

Conclusion: People of "strange talent" may have a special role to fill, precisely because the enemy hasn't built up defenses against them.

As a contemporary application, take scholars who are evangelical and who make their testimony through scholarship in so-called secular fields. They are left-handed Christians. They don't completely fit today's evangelical norm. And those of you who would like to make a contribution through scholarship may sometimes feel a bit doubtful, a bit embarrassed, as if maybe this isn't what you ought to be planning. But God prepares special people to do this special job. You may be one of them.

We read of another group of left-handers in I Chronicles 12:2. At Ziklag, David had some mighty men of Benjamin, helpers in war. They were armed with bows and could use both right and left hands in slinging stones and shooting arrows. They were ambidextrous.

Now a right-handed man seldom builds up his left. But a left-handed man, under psychological pressures, may build up his right. Are you left-handed? By all means become ambidextrous. Learn to witness in a variety of daily situations (but don't fail to put to use that powerful left which God has given you).

Ehud was a judge, and left-handed (Judges 3:15-30). Another Benjaminite. I wonder how many times he had been teased about being a lefty, and how many times he wished that God had made him right-handed so he could be like everybody else.

As Ehud grew up he saw his people in slavery, forced to pay tribute. Then one day the call came to him to do something about it. Do you suppose he objected? "What can I do? I'm not like anybody else. Why don't they call on somebody who's right-handed instead of asking me?"

But Ehud had an idea. He'd capitalize on his difference. He made himself a short sword, strapped it under his clothes on his right thigh, where no ordinary man carried a sword. When his leg moved, the sword moved; it was invisible. Then he selected a gift and with a party of men went to see the king in Moab. With his men he entered the palace, presented his gift and left. But soon he returned alone.

"I have to see the king," he said.

"What's your message? Give it to the secretary."

"I can't do that. It's a secret."

They admitted him to the king's presence, but counselors were there too. So Ehud said, "I have a secret message for you." The men looked him up and down. He was an ordinary-looking person — no sword, no bow, no dagger. So they left.

Then Ehud went close to the king. "Listen!" With his left hand he pulled out the sword. A quick movement, and the fat closed over the blade. Ehud went out, locked the door and left. Finally the bewildered attendants broke in and found the king dead. Israel had peace for 80 years.

Do you feel you're a twisted blade? Too different to be usable by God? Hone this part of your personality to a razor's edge until it is sharp with the Word of God. Use your special experience and develop a way of witness that is effective because it's fresh.

The story of Abraham is worth thinking of over and over again, from various viewpoints. He is, to be sure, the model of an individual maintaining himself as distinct — though alienated — from many of his contemporaries. In the process of individual action, however, he became the initiator of a new social tradition, to which we are heirs.

Abraham, My Father

Abraham kicked a hole through cultural determinism, and opened the door for us to walk through, by faith.

God said to Abraham, "You are a father, Abraham." He called him this before he had a child, because He was going to see to it that there would be a child. The God of Abraham knows what a thing can be, if He calls it to be that. When He says, "Let there be light," there will be light. There does not even have to be the evidence that He is going to fulfill the promise — if there is, in fact, the promise.

We are tempted to be discouraged and quit sometimes when we can't see. But when God says that it is going to rain, you'd better lift up your umbrella, because by the time you get it up, you may be soaked, though you declare it isn't going to rain. By the word of His mouth He called the stars into being — by techniques and processes which are unknown to us. By the word of His power everything came to pass. He spoke and it was done. The communication to us carries with it His purpose and His will, His intent and His promise. It is as good as done.

God called Abraham a father before he was a father. The promise came first. Abraham's body, and that of his wife, were as good as dead, as far as producing children was concerned. He needed a promise for encouragement. Faith without a promise is like a check without a signature.

Then there came obedience. Abraham prepared for a child. But his wife laughed and denied the possibility. It was ridiculous. God then gave them the ability to produce. And so Isaac was born.

We are likely to put the process the other way around. We first have the ability — that is normal. In this instance ability came last. Then there was the test after production. Abraham was tested and tried, and he offered up Isaac. His faith did not stumble; it was greater than mine would have been. He was the first of our cultural genealogy to trust in God in this new resurrection-power sense, thus he is the father of all his successors who believe in this way, both Jews and Gentiles.

Abraham kicked a hole through the cultural determinism of his surroundings by coming out of Ur of the Chaldees and setting up the Hebrew-Christian tradition. He opened the door for us to walk through — by faith.

Whenever anything new is being done it is likely to require some breakthrough like this. The routine, the ordinary task can be handled by routine ability and average techniques. But when a new job is to be done, there must be pioneers because there is no adequate reservoir of history to advise. One must have something like a strong promise, or hope, coupled with courage and obedience. When Abraham was called to go up to a place which he should later receive for an inheritance, he obeyed, and he went out not knowing where he was going. By faith he sojourned in the land, for he looked for a city which has foundations, whose builder and maker is God.

But Abraham and Sarah died in faith. Embarrassingly — for certainty and easy security in faith — they did not get what they believed they had been promised. But they continued to believe that God was eventually going to fulfill the principle of the promise — even after death — in a far greater way than they had dreamed. So they did not turn back. We, too, must take the long view.

We are so far from the kind of events seen in the Old Testament that we are likely to think that if there is a God He must be a deity existing "way out there," far from us. We forget that we are told to pray, "Give us **this** day our daily bread" — and milk and honey. We can ask for new things, today. Now these, in a sense, have been promised. If we seek first the kingdom of God, we have been told, He will give us all else that we need. Since this has been promised, we have the right to ask for it.

Nevertheless, God doesn't always give these things on earth. I am not able to straighten all of this problem out, but I can turn to the book of Hebrews for analogies. We read there in Chapter 11 that some through faith subdued kingdoms, stopped the mouths of lions, escaped the edge of the sword, and thus obtained the promises. But there were others who, not accepting deliverance, were sawn asunder, chopped to pieces, starved to death, and didn't have the clothes they needed. We, too, must be prepared for the alternative — hunger now, joy later — if faith demands this tough trust from us.

We ask for what we need; then we turn to the account concerning Daniel. Three men were told, "You are going to be thrown into the furnace unless you bow down and worship." They answered, "You can't do anything to hurt us. God will take care of us. The Lord will take us out of your hand, Oh King. But **if not** — when we are in that fire, you will have nothing more to say about our bones or our dust. We will be out of your hands and in God's."

> Will we starve to death?
> Okay, we will be with God.
> Will we be martyred?
> Okay — with God.

The promises are eternal. Even Abraham didn't find a city here, but he did later. So we come to limitations on the promise, and I don't know how to handle them all. I just know that for good or ill the promises of God are sure, now or in the life to come.

But how about today? We want to know where to serve and to work. "If you abide in me and I abide in you, you will bring forth fruit that abides forever," is the promise. God will send sap from the roots, up through the branches, to make the plant bear fruit. And He does it even when we can't see it. He calls those things which are not as if they were. In calling them so, He makes them so. He is the God of Abraham, of whom we are heirs, by faith.

And He is at work today in human affairs. As you sleep and as you work, as you get weary and as you learn, as you win or as you lose. He is God, the God of Abraham, and of Isaac, and of Jacob — and of Tom, and of Jane, and of You.

Although the rare pioneering individual like Abraham may add substantially to his culture, most of us do less — and all of us, including the "Abrahams," grow up in a society which teaches us much, forms most of our outlook, and constrains our ordinary patterns of life. Culture is the womb in which we are formed.

Culture, Our Mother

We read in Galatians 4:26 that the Jerusalem which is from above is the mother of us all. In the same context we read that Abraham is our father, the father of those who believe. Abraham had two sons, the one of a bondmaid, the other of a free woman. He who was of the bondwoman was born after the flesh, but he who was of the free woman was by promise.

This metaphor represents the old and the new covenants. The remnant represented by the old woman who could have no child, did have many children, as the stars in the heavens which can't be numbered. Now we, like Isaac, are spiritual children of this promise.

How can we use this figure to illuminate some of our problems today? Abraham is our father, but the Scriptures do not speak of Sarah as our mother. Rather, there is a change of figure to Jerusalem as mother. God is the Author of faith. Abraham, as an individual, believed in Him; the individual involved had to take the initiative. Individualism is relevant in believing; but society is in turn relevant to the believing individual: We are brought up in a cultural matrix.

What is the relation of Christianity to culture? God did not choose individuals only. To many of our contemporaries it is a scandal that there was a chosen nation; but the choice of a social group was no irrelevant accident. A nation was chosen because God wanted to work through the individual **as a member of society.** There can be no role-filled individual without adequate society, nor any adequate society without individuals filling its necessary roles. God, therefore, has never chosen to work with the individual in isolation. He always works with us in the womb of a culture. The personality embryo grows in a cultural setting. This explains for me the whole concept of a chosen people. But this does not support the notion of some of my colleagues who believe in total cultural determinism in which individual illusory choice and initiative become irrelevant. It leaves room for a social structure in which Abraham is our father, and Jerusalem is our mother. The individual stirs and leads us; but society passes on the message. The child needs society.

Several years ago I realized that I had been remiss in the training of my young son. I had not given to our son, through the small nuclear society of our family, the attention to which he was entitled. One day the phone rang and a man said, "Is this the Pike residence?"

"Yes."

"Father of Stephen Pike?"

"Yes."

"Did you know that there was a band concert on tonight that your son was supposed to be playing in?"

I said, "Hold the phone" — and called for his mother. I hadn't known that he was scheduled to be in a concert, but once I heard, I knew it was a serious responsibility. Stephen said that he had stayed home to study. And there he was, watching television, with his bandmaster calling up to know why he wasn't at the concert.

Finally came the message: "This is his teacher, and he is suspended from the band indefinitely."

We were upset because we knew it was important for our boy. He needed the encouragement of the band — it was at the focus of his growth.

I called my boy and said, "Son, you've used up all your excuses. We've tried to let you be adult. We've been ready to reason with you and argue with you, and we've let you persuade us. But evidently we've let you go too far in giving you your freedom, and society has caught up with us."

I took a stick and said, "Bend over, boy," and I let him have it until it hurt us both. I figured I had about a fifty percent chance of saving my fellowship with my son, and yet guide him into a profitable functioning relation with his sub-society. He could have become angry, and rebelled, and hated me forever. But I felt that I had to take that chance because I had been remiss.

Finally — two long days later — my boy said to me, "I don't see why you didn't start this sooner."

A week went by and my wife and I were thanking God for a society which called to our attention where we had not been drawing clearly the boundaries within which, and only within which, a boy could be happy and productive.

As a Christian society we are a team. God in heaven designed that no man will get forgiveness by himself, alone. If you don't forgive your neighbor, God won't forgive you (Matthew 6:15). No man can have a lasting contribution in heaven except it be through the body of Christ — a societal working group. A body needs a heart, and a mind, and feet. It's designed that way. And no man on earth is sufficient of himself. Society is so designed: a chosen nation, a chosen organization, a chosen school, a chosen family. We are not alone. It is not good for man to be alone.

> We sometimes get ready to quit because we see that we are inadequate and unable to do the job. Forgive us, Lord. Help us to see that you never intended us to do anything on our own, but always within society. Help us to serve our institution, our denomination, our colleagues, our family, our nation, the world. Then, Lord, we pray that something might be done that will be fruitful, for Jesus' sake.

To My Son, Stephen:

To help — not hurt;
 To salve, not tear;
Build, not destroy;
 Cure, not kill.

In trouble, we help.
 In sadness, we comfort.
"The bruised reed He will not break,"
 Says the prophet.

God, when finding a person in difficulty,
 Instead of making it worse,
Instead of throwing him away,
 Instead of forcing him to quit —
Even if he has played the fool —
 Wishes to put a splint on his soul
Sending him back to work.

      Love,

        Dad

        Isaiah 42:3

Culture - -

Womb of
Man bound by
Rites.

Words
Come from others —
Some chains are
Tools.

God's
Moral claims
Light freedom's
Way.

You can't write poetry without language; but
language comes from society! Freedom and
truth require moral constraints in personal
structure. Some social controls, like the notes
in music, are needed for the individual to be
able freely to serve the world. This is freedom's
dilemma.

Galatians 4:24-31
John 8:34-36
Judges 12:6
I Corinthians 14:8-11
Philippians 2:7-8

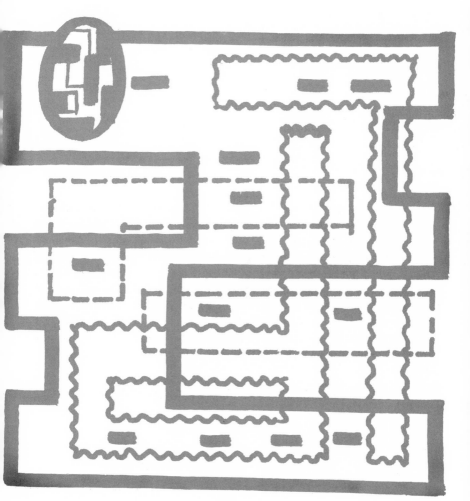

II

THE SCHOLAR
and DILEMMAS

Many problems face the scholar who chooses to be a Christian — or the Christian who trains to be a scholar. With all other men he may have difficulty reconciling his desire for individuality with his longing to merge into and be approved by the group. Or he may be pressed by claims of the society around him, molding him, contributing roles to him. All the while he wishes to determine his own actions. But the scholar may also have some dilemmas which are more especially his own — though these, in principle, are likewise shared to some degree by all.

Intellectual Danger

Where is the scribe?
Where is the wise?
Where is the disputer of this world?
Hath not God made foolish the wisdom of this world?

I Cor. 1:20

These words imply to many of our church friends that intellectualism is dangerous. In the wisdom of God, the world through its wisdom knew not God. It is God's good pleasure to save them that believe through the foolishness of preaching.

But there is a serious problem to be faced. These lines in 1 Corinthians were written by an intellectual, by Paul, who got his "Ph.D." under Gamaliel, the leading scholar of his culture. Paul was a writer — Romans, 1 and 2 Corinthians, Galatians, Ephesians, Philippians, Colossians, 1 and 2 Thessalonians, 1 and 2 Timothy, Titus and Philemon. The colleague who traveled with him was also an intellectual, a medical trainee and the historian who wrote all of Acts and Luke. Between them they wrote some 290 pages out of 467 in the New Testament. If we note the obvious scholarly workmanship on the style of the book of Hebrews, which adds another 18 pages, there are already 308, out of 467, in the New Testament written by intellectuals. On the other hand, the book of John and his three epistles provide 57 pages written by a non-academician. The fisherman — Peter, a tax collector, and a few other authors complete the whole. But the fisherman apparently didn't like to do his own writing so he seems to have called upon a member of a higher social stratum, perhaps academically trained, to present some of his ideas and memoirs.

In the Old Testament the proportion of material written by intellectuals is even greater. Although the book of Psalms, the singing heart of the Bible, was written by a non-academic shepherd (paralleling in this respect the book of John in the New Testament), the bulk of the Old Testament was written by the equivalent of Ph.D.'s. Moses, we have noticed, had 40 years of training in all the learning of the Egyptians. Presumably, therefore, he became competent in oratory, engineering, hieroglyphics, and writing, before he had to learn his spiritual lessons. And

Daniel, in competition with every young scholar of his nation, won a national merit contest along with his three colleagues. He was chosen for an area-study program in the Chaldean language, and in geography, history, and anthropology. We often think of Daniel as a little boy with ruddy cheeks, blushing, refusing to eat anything but a bowl of "oatmeal mush" — how cute! But at the time Daniel was chosen he was at the academic top of his peer group.

Why, then, in 1 Corinthians are there seemingly anti-intellectual statements written by an intellectual? We look at the context and to our astonishment we find that this is a book about Christian society in relation to the time at which Paul wrote. The intellectuals and leaders of the time were the theologians. The problem being attacked by Paul was one of doctrinal legalism and pride. Some were saying, "I am of Paul" (I am of Luther, or Calvin, or Arminius?). It was a set of conflicts within Christian society which was splitting the church of Christ; the clash did not arise from secular science.

Today, there is anti-intellectual bias in much of our Christian culture. With some reason the Christian may be afraid of the intellect. Formerly, in the context of 1 Corinthians, the intellectual threat rose from theological sources. Now the attack is more likely to arise in the context of the universities. The context is different, but the human intellect is the same as ever — dangerous.

Why should the intellect, a great servant, be dangerous? As I see it, every fully logical position, pushed to its bitter (very bitter) end, will eventually lead into trouble, heresy, and chaos. Every logical position is fully consistent, but this coherence arises from the human mind, not God's. The human mind is finite and cannot hold all of eternity in its grasp. If we were able to do so, without contradiction, we ourselves would be God. Our thoughts are not His thoughts. His integrating ability exceeds ours. We find paradox (a polite way of naming logical noncoherence or contradiction) where He knows and sees beautiful fullness of the end from the beginning.

The person who insists on being logical to the end winds up in a mess. I am not saying that we should be irrational. I am not anti-intellectual. I am saying that the intellect by itself is helpless to arrive at **total** truth. We use our intellect, but it

44

has limits. Infinity is in God alone. The logical process carried to the extreme, whether it be in religion or in secularism, is ultimately hostile to humble acceptance of the goodness and wisdom of God.

It is futile by wisdom and by logic to find God. We run into paradoxes. It is only by revelation, and faith in it, that we can find God. He that comes to God must believe that He **is** — and that this makes a difference (Hebrews 11:6).

We know God through Christ. We know truth through Christ. He said, "I am the truth," and then when praying to the Father, "Thy Word is truth." This is central to the nature of truth. Mind and personality are tied together as a man's words flow out from the heart. Out of the heart proceed hatred, murder, adultery, lust, bitterness, and anger — all of these things come out of the heart. Truth also comes out of the heart, if it is there.

We read in Matthew 20 that the disciples of Jesus came to Him asking for an important place. He told them that the way to become great was by serving somebody. He Himself washed the disciples' feet. In Philippians 2 we are told that the Lord Jesus threw away His status and took on the form of a servant. This is what we must do if we want to be great in Christ, without pride of intellect. In 1 Corinthians 12:28 we read that the greater gifts are those for serving, according to the nature of the mind of Christ who gave up status to become a servant. The drive to serve with the intellect and the drive of compassion in the heart must be united for true service. The paradox: Through the intellect of man God has made many of His greatest contributions to us. But if the intellect is not in submission to God, it goes sour, damaging rather than helping. How control it?

> Our Heavenly Father, we realize some of the great dangers of the minds which Thou hast given to us. It was through them that the devil twisted our first parents. We rejoice that the way back to Thee is not through the wisdom of this world, but through the revelation of Thy love. Help us to learn to serve with the mind of Christ who did not serve for status, but served for love.

PRIDE

Vain blockade this —
The haughty snow —
To interrupt
The lava's flow.

How puzzling is pride, appearing in myriad disguises, unknown to the deepest affected, contaminating the committed, resisting the penitent.

The inability of the unregenerate heart — or even the regenerate one — to reform its innersprings of viciousness from which flow bitterness, anger, and corrosive competitiveness is nowhere more clearly seen than here. The attempt of man to revise his own soul is as futile — no matter how beautiful — as the attempt of the new-fallen snow to block the bursting of the hard mountain by a new explosion of lava.

One of the most subtle of all proud wickednesses is the belief that the life of an educated man, a civilized nonsavage, is worth more than the soul of the illiterate peasant of the plains of Mongolia, the savannahs of Africa, or the jungles of Brazil. When did civilization ever control pride, jealousy, envy? Whence the false hope that a full belly will prevent civil war or slashing or fighting in academe?

Only God Himself with His maximum power, the power that raised Christ from the dead, can reach into our inner cesspool.

In spite of dangers with which the wrong use of the intellect threatens us, it is necessary that there be intellectuals. God has used them before, and will again. Some Christians — we might suggest in hyperbole — are tempted to try to resist all academic interests, to sneer and jeer at science, to believe it diabolical at heart. Perhaps, however, an analogy will help these see that, in God's providence, science has a strong contribution for us — whether we like it or not — and that we in turn ought, by God's grace, to contribute to it in our turn.

Captives to Science

On the eve of the Babylonian captivity Jeremiah was having a quarrel with Hananiah and some of the other prophets. Jeremiah said, "Let them take you captive to Babylon." Hananiah said, "No. In two years you will be free." Jeremiah said, "Serve the king of Babylon and live." Hananiah disagreed: "Thus saith the Lord: even so will I break the yoke of Nebuchadnezzar king of Babylon from the neck of all the nations within two years."

Later Jeremiah replied, "Listen, Hananiah. The Lord has not sent you, and you have made this people trust in a lie. Therefore thus says the Lord, 'Behold, I will remove you from the face of the earth. This very year you shall die, because you have uttered rebellion against the Lord.'" In that same year, in the seventh month, the prophet Hananiah died, because he had rebelled against the captivity which God had sent His people.

"But seek the welfare of the city where I have sent you into exile, and pray to the Lord in its behalf, for in its welfare you will find your welfare" (Jeremiah 29:7). Was that the will of God? To serve a foreign government which had led the Jews into captivity, to which they were now slaves? Isn't this being unequally yoked? But Jeremiah had said, "Serve the king of Babylon and live."

We do not ordinarily think of ourselves as captives or in exile, but as I see it, the Christian scholar today is in a difficult captivity which has seldom been equalled in history. It is as grievous to me, I think, as the Babylonian captivity was to the children of Judah. Our captivity today is to science, to the leadership of intellectuals. What a paradox! The living God made knowledge and wisdom, but many of His wishes are rejected — or ignored — by intellectuals who despise Him!

Some of my Christian friends rebel against this exile and say, "No, God will deliver us. God will come in some majestic way and destroy all that these scientists know, with all their power. Just pray and God will destroy the scientists. We can ignore the findings of science. We don't have to go along with these."

I do not believe that this is the way out. If we accept our captivity and serve science, the result will be a witness to scientists, and a feedback into the scientific world, and we shall **live.** We cannot possibly win even the spiritual battle by ignoring science in this generation. We are not going to overcome by a piosity of faith which ignores scientific truth. We are not going to conquer by ignoring what we can see. We must win by serving the king of Babylon, which, I am suggesting, is currently science. Daniel served as a scholar in captivity. Predecessors of the scholars under whom he did graduate work had developed the concept of zero, and other phases of math. They had developed the wheel, and the arch, and many other principles which are used by science today. Daniel served the king of Babylon, and as a servant he was a witness to the cause of Almighty God.

You too may be in some kind of academic captivity and you may be saying, "Yes, I'm a captive — and I don't like it." This is quite irrelevant. Your job is to serve the city by which you have been taken captive, that God might spare it, and our beliefs. This is a part of God's plan to share His Word with the world.

Our Heavenly Father, the words which you gave to Jeremiah were harsh words. Hananiah's words were much more pleasant and congenial. We, too, protest against serving science. And yet, dear Lord, Thou hast made us captive to it in this generation, and we pray that Thou wilt help us. Bless the scientists and linguists, and soften them up to hear the Word. Bless all of them, and open their eyes, for Jesus' sake.

SERVE SCIENCE

I rebel
As slave
To man
(Or God).

Times change —
Once I was
"Free" while
Bound.

Bound, I,
By fact
(In world,
His).

Better,
Far,
"Bound" while
Really free.

Slave, too,
Now (by His plan)
Research exploding
Casts partial light

Truth makes
Free, but
Binds (No lies,
No fake allowed).

On Truth
Of Form
(Planned before
Creation's burst).

As Image, His,
Invent I
(With sweat —
But freely).

'Serve captors or die'
(A tough command).
Science, not Babylon,
Now rides high.

Jeremiah 27:8-17

Pseudo-Immortality

The intellectual merged with preacher in the book of Ecclesiastes. The author was scholar, academician — and depressed. "Vanity of vanities, what's the point of it all," he wants to know. "All things are full of weariness."

He faced a dilemma: He had set his heart on a research career, "to search out wisdom," but everything had already been done. "There is no new thing under the sun." (He couldn't find a new dissertation topic.) So he complained against God and the universe.

A genetically-conditioned demand for seeing cumulative growth drives the scholar. He is not happy unless he finds something new. (Young scholars may thirst to overthrow the past. I myself am living through my second observed linguistic revolution by "young Turks.") Even this is not modern. "For all the Athenians and strangers which were there spent their time in nothing else, but either to tell, or to hear some new thing" (Acts 17:21). The quest for something new was the driving, dynamic force behind that culture which, in a space of a few hundred years, developed, discovered, or discussed almost every conceivable basic philosophical problem. Today it is difficult in philosophy to find anything really new under the sun — the Greeks talked about it first.

In the face of academic ennui the scholar of Ecclesiastes decided to try wine, women, and song (his mind all the while "guiding" him "with wisdom"! — Chapter 2). He built houses, made gardens, had servants, herds, gold, music, and girls in tandem. And yet he wasn't satisfied.

Time passed. The scholar became old; his teeth were gone ("the grinders are few") and his eyes were poor ("windows are darkened"). With a vague homily he tries to tell us to do in our youth what he failed to do in middle age. He couldn't rest satisfied because God had implanted in the genes a desire — which he couldn't seem to locate — for a different kind of fulfillment.

Why the continual unrest?

God has built man so that he is not satisfied unless some-

This essay reprinted by permission of HIS, student magazine of Inter-Varsity Christian Fellowship, © 1967.

thing **lasts.** God has "put eternity into man's mind" (Eccl. 3:11, RSV). Neither you nor I will be satisfied unless we realize that what we are doing today makes, in some sense, a difference forever.

A pseudo-immortality can be sought in various ways. Compare Dan Pedoe's assessment of Buffon's relation to mathematical history: "But he is assured of immortality by his discovery of a beautiful theorem in what is called **geometrical probability.**"[1]

Others wish to achieve a kind of immortality through descendants. The Lord promised it to David, a kingly line through Christ. Still others seek it through passing on property. Here, too, our scholar-cum-businessman was depressed since a fool-and-spendthrift might inherit and dissipate wisdom and goods.

Others seek it in geography, also not new: "They called their lands after their own names" (Psalm 49:11). Note: I did not name Pike's Peak but, curiously enough, enjoy its label.

Nevertheless, as a scholar, I am not particularly interested in getting my name on a mountain peak. My desire is more likely to be connected with a linguistic article. How well I remember the first of my articles to be published in the journal of the Linguistic Society of America, **Language:** "Taxemes and Immediate Constituents," by Kenneth L. Pike. I ordered a bunch of reprints with covers. (You pay extra for those clean yellow covers!) The editor told me that he bought paper guaranteed to last 500 years. My own pseudo-eternity! I didn't know what would happen to my article after 500 years, but until then I'd be all right, maybe.

I was in an Indian village in Mexico when the reprints reached me, and I stacked them in a spot in the tool shed that I had turned into an office. I put "Taxemes and Immediate Constituents" on a nice cleaned-out spot on a storage shelf there.

Then one day I wanted to send a copy to a scholar whom I hoped to interest in the material. I reached up and pulled one down. I looked at it. There were two holes in it! So I put it aside annoyed. With a feeling of hurt (oh my child!) I pulled down another one. And there were holes in that one, too. A five-hundred-year guarantee and holes in it already! I took the rest down and found that termites had stitched holes back and

1. The Gentle Art of Mathematics, Penguin (1958) 1963, p. 59.

forth through the whole pack. There were termites in the article that was going to give me 500 years of eternity.

How deeply we want immortality—and how easily we accept fleeting substitutes. Even a small public notice of our name may satisfy us. Ernest Hemingway said: "In those days (when he was a young man in Paris) many people went to the cafés at the corner of the Boulevard Montparnasse and the Boulevard Raspil to be seen publicly and in a way such places anticipated the columnists as the daily substitutes for immortality."[2]

But God, who through our genetic equipment put into us an unquenchable thirst crying for eternity, will give each of His children an eternal name—a private name no man knows except the one who receives it, given by God to characterize what he really is. A stamp of genuineness that he is himself, and eternally valuable.

Me, an individual, not merged into fog, or dust, or even undifferentiated spirit or goodness or power. Me! Named by God, forever.

2. A Moveable Feast, New York, 1964, p. 81.

Another dilemma may face the younger scholar: often he feels that his training implies an eternal commitment to a particular task — (or at least a life-long investment, which at the moment may seem long enough!). But the tug at his interests, or compassion, or the available places for work, may appear to lead to the loss of the investment in that training. He finds it hard to realize that many scholars have shifted fields and jobs with gain — not loss. The crucial personality invariant is the permanently molded character of the trained man — not the few concepts temporarily in his head.

Yours ≠ You

How
>can I change my job

Lose
>the years of work invested

Fail
>my dreams of role fulfilled?

Dump
>all that?

Moses —
>(Orator-Engineer)

Daniel —
>(Area Specialist)

Paul —
>(Expert in the Law)

Training,
>"used"?? — **why?**

Yours —
>degree, talent, this-and-that;

You —
>psyche, mind, guts.

God —
>turns shepherd heart to King.

Role —
>grows from **man** — not robot.
>>Training ≠ Call

Acts 7:22; Daniel 1:4-6; 2:19
Acts 22:3, 18; Galatians 2:9

55

In the preceding essay we saw that the scholar was seeking a positive element — a kind of eternity — but in an inadequate fashion. Here, I point to a negative element in the report — a gap in his struggle. Nowhere could I find the faintest trace of trying to help **someone else.** He was lustful of knowledge solely for his own interest; he trembled at the future of his lands only for his own name; his success or failure was calibrated by what it did for him, not others.

He failed to see in advance, that which Paul might have taught him later (1 Corinthians 12 and 13), that the greatest gift is not flashy ability, not even academic or deep spiritual insight, but love, service, and consideration for others.

It is not good for man to be alone. The individual needs linkage with society. But linkage fruitful to the soul must come from service to others, even as the Son of Man came not to be ministered unto, as a king, but to minister. Poor man. Either he didn't know that, or sinned in brushing it aside. The dilemma: to get the deepest joy one must give until it hurts.

The Disillusioned Scholar

For each of our roles the Lord has particular warnings. What are those for the scholar? I turn again to the book of Ecclesiastes to illustrate a further point. In this book there is some very good advice: "Whatever your hand finds to do, do it with your might" (9:10). Or, "In the morning sow your seed, and at evening withhold not your hand: for you do not know which will prosper, this or that, or whether both alike will be good" (11:16). These have condemned me — and blessed me — but even put together they fail to illuminate for me the purpose of the book as a whole.

As I see it, perhaps from a particularly biased perspective, this book meets one crucial need of the disillusioned theistic scholar. Occasionally you see on campus the deep personal hurt of scholars in a dilemma: they can't give up their moral structure and can't give up their Christianity, but don't quite know how to make it fit into their intellectual life. They may even have become "hidden" Christian professors. And at times I am tempted to become one of them, so this book is written for me also.

This theistic scholar, the wise man of his society, had a deep struggle to make sense out of his academic data, while retaining faith in God. He almost lost it. In the process his personal life became chaos. "So I hated life" (2:17). When he was an old man, an old scholar, when he could not run around or "play around" any more, he says, "Now remember God" (12:1).

His struggle as scholar was to make honest sense of **personal** data while retaining faith in God, as Job's struggle was to make honest sense of the **moral** universe while retaining faith in the same God.

In chapter one the scholar is in utter depression about the dull repetitiveness of life, until all he wants to do is scream, and drop it all — but he can't quite do it. One generation passes away, another comes. The sun goes down, the sun comes up. The wind goes this way, the wind goes that way. Everything that happens has happened once before.

A "tired" scholar! No matter how much he sees and learns, he can never be satisfied. Everything that will be done has been done, he sighs, and yet I am a research scholar looking for something new.

It is hard today for the non-academician, who sees new space ships, new explosions, new research institutes, to understand how **even now** the same drabness and weariness of repetition can affect a twentieth-century professor. But space ships can appear to the disenchanted as merely bigger rockets pushed on by centuries-old principles and long-known formulas. Even the very search for newness itself can become old and soul-empty. (Who, eventually, could be satisfied with being **always** engaged but **never** married, **always** searching for ultimate truth but **never** finding rest in it?) The scholar writes his book, but the making of it is a weariness to the flesh, if after he has published it somebody says, "Oh it's been done in principle before," which, in some sense, it always has.

I had a young Ph.D. in my office a few years ago who said that he had chosen a new brand of linguistic theory because he wanted something that would stand true forever, and wouldn't have to be done over again. What he wanted, above everything else, was to do something **cumulative** and **new** that would last forever. And he was already disillusioned with other theories which appeared doomed.

The curious paradox: The scholar of Ecclesiastes sought to avoid pain, but ended with mental anguish. Paul chose service, accepted pain, and through weakness became strong in God. Death is swallowed up in new life. Deep service costs pain. Whereas for nothing one gets nothing.

II Corinthians 12:8-12
4:16-17; 11:12-29

THORNS HURT

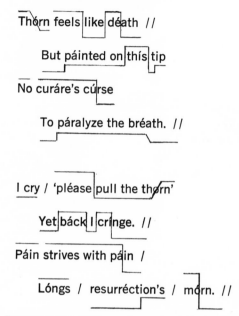

Thórn feels like déath //

But páinted on thís tip

No curáre's cúrse

To páralyze the bréath. //

I cry / 'pléase pull the thórn'

Yet báck I crínge. //

Páin strives with páin /

Lóngs / resurréction's / mórn. //

Can you whistle? Follow the line slowly — a four-note staff. Pause 'poised' at
/. Pause 'relaxed' at //. Then talk normally to this tune. Don't drop the pitch
at the end of line 5.

The paradox: Excessive tension can destroy us — this must be avoided. But without tension we, like a flaccid violin string, can serve no one.

tension

String — taut stretched —
Snap not! Nor grieve
When frightful bow draws
Forth the haunting fear.
Please, Lord, play on.

2 Cor. 12:9

63

Mental Tension

Paul told us that we would pass through much tribulation in entering the Kingdom of God (Acts 14:22).

When we look for the twentieth-century equivalent of what we normally consider to be tribulation, we at first fail to find it, for most of us — few of us — suffer persecution unto death. Yet the principle must somehow be universal, since we are all alike in our basic struggle and temptations (I Corinthians 10:13). Of course during times of war, even now, there is physical tribulation, and in some tribal areas Christians face hunger and other physical trials. But most of us experience the tribulation that Paul talks about through mental tension. It is important that we understand this, because when we do, we can bring the same tools to bear on mental tension that allow people to survive physical trials.

We have been told so often that a Christian is radiant and joyful that we consider ourselves sinners when we are sad and weary. Probably we are, but all through the book of Second Corinthians we find Paul almost to the breaking point with mental anxiety. "We are pressed out of measure, above strength, in so much that we despaired even of life." Perhaps at this point he was in physical danger from the lions (cf. I Corinthians 15:32), but the book goes on, "We have this treasure in earthen vessels . . . we are troubled on every side . . ."

There is no escape from mental anxiety and tension. There are tools with which to try to meet it, but no real way to keep from "dying." We must die to ourselves, die to our wishes, die to our hopes, die to the point at which we are willing to accept tension. Once we have found that we are powerless, and unable to do a job which is our responsibility, we are more likely to call on God to do it. He is able.

Some of our mental tensions come from sickness in the family, some from personal relationships with colleagues, some from studies, some from trying to make choices as to which job has priority, some because we feel inadequate. There is no escape from tension. We must embrace it. Not because we like it, but because through it we can "die"; because through it we learn that "except a grain of wheat fall into the ground and die, it abideth alone" (John 12:24). There is no easy road whereby we can make a contribution to others. I haven't found any — nor does the Scripture promise any. Somebody may have to get hurt if somebody else is going to be helped. It is the law of life that he that would save his life and take an easy spot where he is not under stress, will lose his life. He will amount to absolutely nothing. But he that is ready to lose his life — including the acceptance of mental tension — will live, and will help somebody else to live also (II Corinthians 4:12).

Accept a measured degree of unavoidable stress (but — the dilemma — do not be silly by holding unnecessarily to stress-making situations you cannot survive). When it "kills" you, you can trust in God. Only when we trust in God can we get work done, because "except the Lord build the house, they labor in vain that build it" (Psa. 127:1). Only when we have enough mental stress to force us to see our bankruptcy of power do we trust in God, and only when we trust in God can we make our eternal contribution which will not collapse. "It is vain for you to rise up early . . . for so he giveth his beloved sleep" (Psa. 127:2). Hard work is not enough.

If we would contribute to others, we must have the courage to face tension, and to accept the death which it brings.

Under tension, a person may wish to give up the struggle. It can happen to the most effective of God's servants, even after successful work. Without effective results, one may become depressed. But — a strange paradox — depression may come under the opposite conditions when energy has been well spent.

Tempted to Quit

Elijah "went a day's journey into the wilderness, and came and sat down under a juniper tree: and he requested for himself that he might die; and said, It is enough; now, O Lord, take away my life; for I am not better than my fathers" (I Kings 19:4). And he lay and slept.

Elijah's death wish came right after he was successful. That is a strange time! Perhaps you are more likely to have yours when you are **un**successful; but no temptation reached Elijah except such as is common to man. If it hasn't hit you yet, it will.

Job was in quite different circumstances. He had the itch-and-scratch, and as he sat on the ash heap trying to comfort himself he said, "Let the day perish wherein I was born" (He said it much more poetically than Elijah did.) "May God above not seek it, nor lights shine upon it" (Job 3:3-4) — on and on.

Where did his wish come from? From the **unfairness** of the world, whereas Elijah's wishing he could die was due to **exhaustion** — not sinfulness. It was not a blatant sinner who said there, "Lord, let me die." It was a courageous saint a moment after the hour of his triumph. When someone touched the hem of Jesus' garment, He felt energy leave Him, and said, "Somebody touched me." But they said, "Nobody touched you." And he replied, "Oh? I felt an energy loss." None of us as men can do any good to anybody without paying a price — without losing energy. And if we try to do much good, and if we succeed, we pay a lot.

Elijah, when he wished he were dead, was exhausted emotionally and physically. He had run down from the mountain ahead of the chariot — that's a pretty good race, even down hill — and he was physically tired. He was also emotionally exhausted. He had taunted and teased the prophets of Baal because their god couldn't do anything. Then he got by himself and prayed, "Lord, send fire." And he waited (but suppose God didn't answer!). That must have taken emotional energy. And then when, after all of this, Jezebel wanted to find him and cut his throat, it was the last straw. He fled in sheer exhaustion.

With Job it was the knowledge that "the robbers prosper" that wearied him. When you are doing what is right, and you are accused of being wrong, that can hurt more deeply than almost anything else.

On the other hand, the scholar, the disillusioned theistic scholar of Ecclesiastes, was not troubled as Job was by the unfairness of the universe morally. Nor did he collapse as Elijah did from physical and emotional exhaustion. Rather, he nearly disintegrated from **mental** exhaustion — the sheer hopelessness of ever arriving at anything which appeared to be cumulative. And so he hated life because what is done under the sun was grievous to him.

It isn't polite to admit that sometimes you too, as a Christian, wish that the "whole thing" were over, or that you could "get out of" your task. So we have to translate the word "die" into the word "quit," before it is easier to discuss. Perhaps half of us have at some time wished we could quit our work. Even Jesus said, "My Father, if it be possible, let this cup pass from me; nevertheless not as **I will** but as thou wilt" (Matt. 26:39).

"Father, glorify thy name." He chose **against temptation,** to be a "grain of wheat" — to do His job.

Compare, also, Paul's inner struggle, seen in II Corinthians 5:1-2. "For we know that if the earthly tent (our body) . . . is destroyed, we have a building from God (a resurrected body), a house not made with hands, eternal . . . Here indeed we groan, and long to put on our heavenly dwelling." And, he says, "For to me to live is Christ, and to die is gain," but "if it is to be life in the flesh, that means fruitful labor for me. Yet which I shall choose I cannot tell. I am hard pressed between the two. My desire is to depart and be with Christ" (Philippians 1:21-23).

In the dilemma he chose not to quit. What is the difference between wishing you were dead to be with Christ and just wishing you were dead? It is the difference between a Christian and a drunk. The drunk drinks to get oblivion — to forget. The Christian wishes he were out from under the trouble — to have conscious, abundant, victorious, sinless life. There are other names for it; a lovely one appears in Hebrews 4:9: "There remains a sabbath rest for the people of God." A rest in which there will be no more struggle to be good!

TO BE

Good,
    As birds fly by the stars;
    And homing pigeon
    Comes back to nest!

Good —
    Because "built in,"
    Written on tables of the heart.
    That will be
Rest.

Jeremiah 31:33
Isaiah 1:3
Hebrews 4:9-10

Meanwhile — in struggle and in dilemma — we trust to God's guidance. He knows the way, because He is the way.

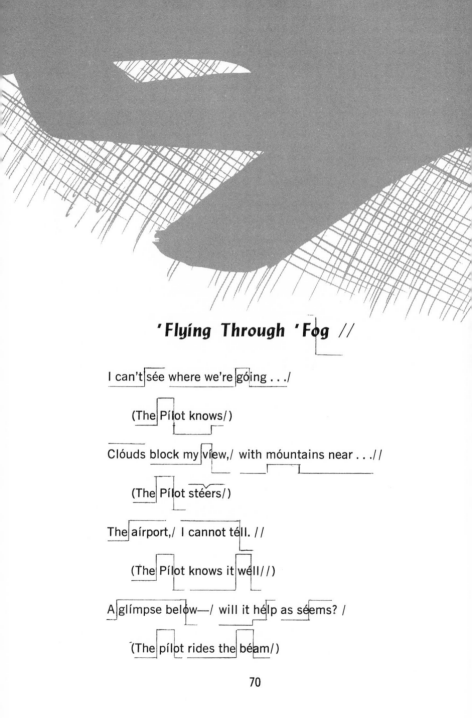

′Flying Through ′Fog //

I can't sée where we're góing . . ./

    (The Pílot knows/)

Clóuds block my víew,/ with móuntains near . . .//

    (The Pílot stéers/)

The aírport,/ I cannot téll. //

    (The Pílot knows it wéll//)

A glímpse belów—/ will it hélp as séems? /

    (The pílot rides the béam/)

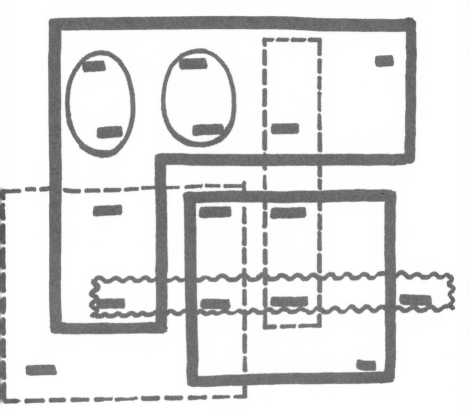

III

THE SCHOLAR
and SOCIAL ISSUES

STRENGTH

Strength — measured by
Napoleon, Hitler, Khan
Or student power to wreck.

Weakness — of
Love, joy, meekness,
Or student peace corps.

What price
Glory? Eternal treasures lie
In men alone — my neighbor served for
Christ — who gives that
Light, goodness, gentleness, which
Kings and Scholars thirst for.
Drink!

God in History

Before discussing problems which confront him, and the claims upon him, the Christian first affirms that God rides the storm; God operates in history in ways inscrutable. We feel whipsawed between pain and joy, while believing that God is there working mysteriously through both. Problems, pain, sins, joys, victories — between the mess and the glory, all in one, we oscillate. Strange hybrid creatures that we are, to us in the midst of darkness and sin, mixups and quarrels, comes the grace of God.

Isaiah shows us the problem. "The ox knows its owner, and the ass its master's crib; but Israel does not know; my people do not understand" (1:3). God built us to know Him, as He built the bees to fly from the comb to the flowers and to return, then to go through a little dance by which they send their sisters out to the very place they found nectar. God built us, that by **instinct** we **ought** to obey Him — but He added the power to refuse. And we chose to refuse. The ox knows his owner, he has a built-in ability to learn to recognize authority. The ass knows his master's crib; he knows how to go home. But we don't know how to go home; we don't know how to recognize our Owner, Boss, Creator. What is wrong?

Sociologically: "Seek justice, correct oppression; defend the fatherless, plead for the widow" (Isa. 1:7). Sociological catastrophe. Lack of justice. Civil rights not met. When you get outside of the United States — which is **relatively** just, let me assure you — you may find injustice that you can't even cry out against (you have no valid voice). From within the horror and the mess you can only cry to God.

Psychologically: Guilt. "Come now, let us reason together . . . your sins are as scarlet" (Isa. 1:18). Genuine guilt. Not just something unfortunate, not something to be ignored, not something to be repressed, but something to be verbalized — but verbalized to God. "I'm wrong, I'm dirty, and I need to be washed."

Politically: "And the daughter of Zion is left like a booth in a vineyard, like a lodge in a cucumber field, like a besieged city" (Isa. 1:8). In a culture such as that was (and such as I also have for a time lived in) thieves come and strip the corn off the stalk when it is ripening. In order to guard the crop, you must build yourself a little hut, just big enough to crawl into at night, and sleep there. If there is any noise, you get up, pace around, and drive away the animals (two-legged or four-legged). But when the city itself is under siege, you cannot sleep alone outside the wall. So the little hut is abandoned with its crops, its fruit, its food, its life, in order for the moment to allow one to care for the mere body which later will die without the food which should have been protected by the little lodge in the cucumber patch. And along with the big hunger come political chaos and collapse.

Religiously: Futility, hypocrisy. See the message in Isaiah 1:11. To what purpose is the multitude of your spiritual-sounding phrases, your spiritual-looking exercises, your prayer meetings? What is the purpose of the multitude of your sacrifices? God doesn't want any more when you choose to be unjust. To assume that you are "spiritual" when you are "orthodox" but cheat or hate your brother is a lie, a stench, a spiritual mess.

Historically: Mess. "How the faithful city has become a harlot" (Isa. 1:21). That city which used to serve God with justice and righteousness now has become a den of thieves. The princes are rebellious; administration has collapsed; bribery has come in; companions of the judges are crooks, gangsters have taken over the judicial system.

Yet we can begin to see through the clouds to glory beyond, the glory, as promised in 1:26-27: "I will restore thy judges as at the first." Selfless administration will be reestablished. Impurity will be taken away. "Afterward you shall be called the city of righteousness, the faithful city. Zion shall be redeemed by justice, and those in her who repent, by righteousness."

If there is tension within us as we try to reconcile faith in God's goodness with observation of the chaos, we can try to reconcile this tension in two different ways. On the one hand, we can deny the mess (or deny that God allows any evil) and claim that there is no danger to the innocent (Job 4:7). On the other hand we can say with Job: "I see the robbers prospering" (cf. 12:6). "This is what I see; if God collapses by my telling the truth, He will have to collapse." Eliphaz counters: "You are destroying knowledge of God" (15:4). Job implies, "Don't try to steady the ark. If God collapses because of the truth, He had better collapse. He must face all truth because He is the author of all truth." (Cf. 13:8, 10.) But Eliphaz feels this hinders belief in God (15:4).

Let us admit the truth. There **is** mess. But beyond that mess lies redemptive glory for us.

In the next ten years it will continue to be difficult to reconcile faith in God with observation of mess, injustice, and tension — between us and our colleagues, between us and the world, between the people we are working with and their governments. It will be hard to see how God is at work **there.** The book of Isaiah, perhaps above all other books, shows the need for a stereoscopic view of the world: through our secular eye (mess and problems), and through our spiritual eye (glory waiting behind the same thing). When we put the views together we see God in history, God working. This faith, and this alone, may carry some of us through the next decade with happiness.

For international problems we may need to build bomb shelters. "Enter into the rock and hide in the dust from before the terror of the Lord" (Isa. 2:10). (That sounds up-to-date.) Where is shelter? The Lord is going to bring judgment. "When the Lord shall have washed away the filth of the daughters of Zion and cleansed the bloodstains of Jerusalem from its midst by a spirit . . . the Lord will create over the whole site of Mount Zion and over her assemblies a cloud by day, and smoke and the shining of a flaming fire by night" (Isa. 4:4-5). God Himself will build shelter: "For over all the glory there will be a canopy and a pavilion. It will be for a shade by day from the heat, and for a refuge and a shelter from the storm and rain" (Isa. 4:5-6).

Behind history lies a Person. He, God, is **there.** God is at work **now,** in current events, in kings, prices, revolts, rebellions. How, I don't know, but I believe it. I affirm it, although I can't prove it.

And in His hand lies the breath of every tyrant, to be stopped.

"The power is mine,"
    The tyrant chants.
Yet he pants;
    Breath comes short.
God squeezes.
    Sovereign sneezes...
        And poof!

Intergenerational Cleavage

Both old and young deplore the problems of our modern world. But they see them differently. Each feels that the other is seeing through intellectual prisms which distort reality to right or to left. These differences — viewpoints — called by some of them intergenerational cleavage, I have recently had occasion to observe as a faculty member of the University of Michigan.

Activist students are taking part more in university outlook, administration, and decision. I have been attempting to understand the upheaval as I never have before. I have tried to understand their protests, their sit-ins, and their solid contributions to the community. To me, not necessarily to them, this unrest implies a longing **thirst for meaning.**

They strive to see relevance in life. This struggle ties them to society in three directions. It ties them hostilely. They attack society because they want freedom from it. They want freedom from its moral controls, except as they set rules. They want freedom from belonging. They don't want to have to fit; they protest continuously against it. They want freedom from its government, except as they comprise it.

Out of this latter wish grows another link: They are tied to society positively by a vigorous attempt to build it. They want student forms of society. They want forms of society which are built around them, which they themselves vote on. But in addition they want forms of society which go outside themselves. They demonstrate for civil rights, for justice, and for service. On one hand the activists may try to disassociate themselves from society because it makes them feel too cramped, and on the other hand to build up a society to which they think they would like to belong.

In the process there is an astonishing shift from the moral stance of my own generation. Some of the academic thrust of my contemporaries was an attempt to teach a complete moral relativity, in which standards were derived exclusively from man's culture (God and His orders were considered non-existent). The dominant theme was cultural relativity, which led to individual relativity in morals. The astonishing change, as I seem to sense it, is the underlying, implicit repudiation of this stance (while retaining it in words from a former generation).

I am not at all sure how many of the students or my university colleagues would grant this point. The main reason is that while there is still a repudiation of absolutes in terms of personal morals (often centering around sex), there are other issues which are widely proclaimed. The activist may insist that these are **the** genuine moral issues in which the community should be involved, while refusing the same treatment to disagreements over society's right to protest against sexual license. This shift, narrowing the scope of the moral scene but at the same time heightening the intensity of its relevance, confuses us. **The surge towards a demand for absolute justice can grow only in a soil inoculated against** the absolutes of **total relativity.**

After a large protest meeting of about 4000 students in the spring of 1967 at the University of Michigan, the president of the University appointed a student commission to consider problems. Roger Leed, the student member of this commission on decision-making, stated: "The participatory democracy emphasis is an element of the Movement's general concern with elevating moral issues to equal dignity with any other type of issue" ("Students and University Decision-Making": Guild House, 1967).

Students are also interested in freedom as a moral issue. This freedom is then often defined in reference to students making moral, social, and political judgments about what concerns **them.** This freedom purports to allow a man to vote as to what kind of society he would like — but at the extreme, makes no commitment as to **how large** a segment of society is involved in group commitment or what to do with minority refusal. After an Administration-Building sit-in in late 1966, several students were interviewed to ascertain: "What is behind the applause that speeches about 'student power' have been receiving on the U-M campus? **(The Ann Arbor News,** Dec. 7, 1966). One student was asked:

Q — What do you think "student power" should mean at the U-M?

A — "Any decision about student life should be made by students. If, for example, students decided women should be able to spend Saturday nights in the men's dormitories, I think that would be a legitimate decision. Most universities have better rules for dormitories than the U-M."

A handout prepared by radical activists given to me at a mass meeting of 4000 students says: "We must understand that we have no moral responsibility to obey rules made **for** us by the administration. It is one of the most basic assumptions of both liberal and radical political theory that sovereignty and the right to decide must reside in those affected by the decisions made."

Students are claiming access to decision-making as a moral right, on moral grounds, in moral terms, towards the building of a good society. In the handout referred to above is the statement:

"As students, we should be seeking a meaningful life for ourselves, a chance to develop into self-directing, free human beings. Career-training is of course vital, but neither job nor education is worth much to the individual or to the building of a decent society unless that job or education helps the individual to develop his own potential in his own way. In contrast with administrative socialization, the process of self-development requires student freedom. But the freedom of students denies the freedom of the administration to mold us in the image of the present society. Some of us might choose to develop in that direction on our own, but that choice must be our own. We must also have the opportunity to develop into opponents of the present structure of society and to use our years as students to help develop structures more hospitable to meaningful human life."

Some students object to being molded to fit society's machine. They wish to leave that for IBM punch cards. They want to be free; they want to be individuals; they want to be different. In a brochure distributed by the radical Students for a Democratic Society a protest against this type of standardization is registered: "Both student and teacher are tool and product of administrative totalitarianism. The student comes out of high school a finished product to be consumed by either the agro-business or the war machine. He is by then also a tool, to be used to make others conform. The teacher, who began as a tool in an Orwellian nightmare finally believes that he is helping his students to lead useful and moral lives in our society" ("High School Reform: Towards a Student Movement," by Students for a Democratic Society, Feb. 1966).

The large majority of students are not anti-society, but may adopt purely humanistic value systems. The retiring managing editor of **The Michigan Daily,** Kenneth Winter, wrote on April 13, 1965, in an editorial entitled "The Search for Valid Standards": "The basically true standard, it seems to me, is people: the values, the desires, the aspirations, the needs — in short, the happiness — of present and future generations of human beings. Other standards are true only if and when they contribute to this standard."

In my view, the needs of people — of our near and of our remote neighbors — are indeed crucial to any ethic. But this ethic is truncated if it is presented as involving only man with man. A solid platform can eventually be built only in reference to the will and character of God, who demands that I love my neighbor. Obedience to the larger Power — and strength derived then from Him — counteracts some of my inbuilt selfishness separating me from service to society.

nothing from everything

Pop gave me "everything"
But I have nothing.
 What good is freedom
 of time from sweat;
What serves car and cash
If goal is crash?
 I didn't learn — nor he tell —
 Joy means giving, not getting;
Better less fun, more service,
Off wheel of boredom 'under the sun.'
 Stop! Take direction —
 And course correction.
Not yet too late.
Just skip that date.

Ecclesiastes 1:9; 2:1
Acts 20:35
Proverbs 11:24; 15:17

If happiness is too narrowly interpreted, boredom comes even with riches. Only on a deep personal and social moral foundation — driving one to service for others — can the full life be built. This, in turn, needs theistic source for ultimate effectiveness.

YOUNG ROBOTS

There was an editorial in the **Michigan Daily** on November 23, 1966, written by Bruce Wasserstein and Harvey Wasserman, dealing with the problem of the university administration and the House Unamerican Activities Committee, which summed up the freedom debate thus: "Whether it be the HUAC issue, police on campus, the bookstore, the sit-in ban, or the draft referendum, the fundamental problem is that students don't have real power in governing their own lives."

On these grounds the (official) Student Government Council this past year declared itself free from the administration (which supports it financially, provides buildings and other equipment). Michael Heffer said in the **Michigan Daily,** March 26, 1967: "Several students awaiting final approval of their membership on the Joint Judiciary Council predict that in the future the judiciary will acquit all students charged with violating rules established by administrators or established by students when administrators had veto power over them."

Reaction to administrative control was further reported in the **Michigan Daily,** April 7, 1967: "The University is turning out bright young robots, charged Ed Robinson, '67, former president of the Student Government Council, at yesterday's meeting of the Presidential Committee on the Role of the Student in Decision-Making."

All of this leads to some peculiar problems. In order to effect change, the far-out radicals seem to be ready to disrupt and to destroy. Members of the Students for a Democratic Society tried to disrupt a meeting featuring Senator Philip Hart, Michigan Democrat, and House Minority Leader Gerald Ford of Grand Rapids, in Ann Arbor on March 2, 1967. The incident was reported in the **Ann Arbor News,** March 18, 1967, with the following reaction from the Graduate School:

"Members of the community of scholars have the responsibility for respecting and protecting the rights of others to express their views.

"The Executive Board of the Graduate School deplores the actions of a group of individuals at a public meeting held by the University of Michigan in the Rackham Lecture Hall on March 2 which resulted in a clear infringement of these rights."

That is, the Graduate School took the view that part of the essential training given to a graduate student is to teach him to listen to other people and their views. Disruption of a lecture, therefore, became specifically an academic matter, within their direct purview and control.

Thus freedom comes into clash with freedom. The Good Society cannot allow perfect freedom to absolute selfishness. Somewhere a balance must be struck, lest new tyrannies replace old ones under freedom's banner. The desire to escape robotism must be tempered with care lest others be placed under unwilling control.

One-Way Street?

Justice is all I ask —
Give me mine!

Claim not yours —
That, too, I hold.

Don't plead for fairness.
Right's for **me** — Not you!

We find it much easier to see
that our neighbor is unreasonable
(when he treads on our lawn)
than we do to see our damage to him
(when we make a path through his hedge).

Student Power

(Smash, grind, stomp!)
'I don't like your world —
Go 'way!'
(Stir, change, create!)
'I don't like our world —
Help build it.'

FLAMING CREATURES

Two issues get mixed: (1) The need for positive action to change the world for good; (2) The need for positive action to prevent the world from being changed for worse. We disagree as to where they begin, end, and crisscross.

As for me, I applaud the search for development of the rights and organizational structures of underprivileged people. For thirty years I have consistently spent much time, effort, travel, and direct involvement in trying to serve small tribal groups (outside the U.S.A.) — so small that most civil rights movements at home or abroad could pass them by, noticing neither the omission nor its inconsistency. Much less frequently I have attempted to suggest caution, to members of my own culture, when damage to it appeared probable.

Recently, for example, the issues of freedom of personal moral responsibility, and of encroaching public indecency got mixed with the issue of academic freedom. It appeared to me that valid testing of areas of legal freedom and responsibility was degenerating into an attack on decency. A film called "Flaming Creatures" had been shown on campus, through a student organization. A police officer interrupted a showing of the film, and confiscated it, because of its obscene nature. This exploded into a legal problem — not settled at the time of writing — involving his right to do so.

Various persons writing in the student newspaper, however, discussed more directly the moral issues involved — the majority of them defending the film, either — it seemed to me — by an implied attack on morals as such, or by attempting to defend the film as being artistic, or as an esthetic experiment, or by affirming that the offending part (like a "small" worm in a nice apple, I suppose) was only a small part of the whole — and hence, the whole should not be judged obscene by contamination. Members of the University of Michigan Alumni Wrestling Club (whom I have no reason to suspect are nonvirile judges), on the other hand, were "outraged and incensed" by the showing of the film, and wrote to the editor of the **Michigan Daily,** February 22, 1967: "The film is beyond a doubt pornographic, lewd, an insult to all human dignity and below the realm of moral decency . . . The film goes well beyond the limits of academic freedom that can be tolerated on the University campus . . . The showing of 'Flaming Creatures' goes even beyond the writing of obscene words on lavatory walls."

I finally decided to join the discussion with a bit of satire or parable. This form I chose, because I could not handle the direct analysis of the **definition** of obscenity—that is hard enough to give pause to the courts. I thought, however, that I could make my actual position clear enough for any who chose to read, by showing that innocent dogs and doves are — or are not — restrained from contaminating our environment. Surely we could expect no less from students? In addition, good things of life — roast beef (or sex) — can all be distorted to corruption; an artistic label on written or filmed garbage should not make it more palatable or socially acceptable.

The letter, which I append to this essay ("After all, doves fly overhead"), was rejected by the editor of the **Michigan Daily.** I therefore purchased advertising space in the **Daily,** and published it there (March 12, 1967).

I then submitted a further letter to the editor, which was published on March 14 (appended, also, below, "Paper's Power" — title added by the editor). Here the issue was different. The Board in Control of Student Publications had refused to appoint, as in-coming editor of the paper, a nominee (the "hero" in my letter) of the outgoing staff of the **Daily** (including the then editor, Mark Killingsworth). The staff felt there was no adequate basis for this refusal. Someone — not mentioned in the **Daily** — informed the legislators in Lansing whereupon 35 of them (the "posse") signed a telegram which was followed by a reversal of the Board's position, and the election of the editor as previously nominated.

Later I was able to talk with some of the people involved in such discussions. I told them that I believed the current generation was demanding a kind of moral security which they had — unfortunately — not been given by our generation. I declared that their protest at injustice implied belief in an implicit, quasi-absolute underlying moral code, which at times they were, nevertheless, denying — their agitation was built on a moral base. If we could get this widely affirmed publicly, I felt, we could then more effectively encourage constructive good.

I was especially impressed by the farewell editorial of the outgoing editor of the **Michigan Daily,** Mark R. Killingsworth, who stated, April 14, 1967, in recapitulation of the issues: "The real reason, I'm afraid, why teachers don't involve their students in their class, why administrators shy from consulting students (and faculty), is that they don't love them: that they don't have the kind of trust and feeling about them which even understands weakness and folly and error which love inspires — or, if they do have that feeling, they are too afraid to act on it.

"Too often the feeling is instead one of distrust, a belief that 'rules must be followed, because if we don't have any, people might get out of hand,' a 'haunting fear,' as H. L. Mencken put it, that 'somebody, somewhere might be happy.'

"Perhaps that criticism equally applies to **The Daily** and its critics. For I suspect **The Daily's** greatest weakness is not its inaccuracy or its unfairness in attacking its enemies — in all honesty I think we have surprisingly little of that. Rather, we don't love them enough."

To the Editor of the Michigan Daily

After all, doves fly overhead,
dropping what, where, when they please —
Why not students?

Or should both doves and students
be issued trash bins?
Otherwise why should we protest
against a student walking, leaving,
dropping a candy wrapper
without look to right or left,
without a flutter of a wing?

How impossible to meet the demand
to define the line
where freedom meets license!

At what moment does a piece of prime roast beef
Turn to garbage?
Under this snare — say the demand
for Definition of "garbage" —
How can it be recognized when
it occurs in a jewelled setting
(to mix metaphors,
as self-respecting garbage should)?

After all, dogs like freedom to delve in garbage cans,
spew and strew over neighbors' lawns as they please—
why not students?

Or should both be given license?
Both innocent creatures and Flaming Creatures?

Paper's Power

To the Editor:

TRAMP, TRAMP, the footprints of 35 vigilantes crossed the pages of The Daily. Not, of course, "Moral Vigilantes" of the policeman type castigated by Mr. Killingsworth (Feb. 25) for their "brutish sensibilities." Oh no, no — those would be black hats. It's the white hats in defense of conscience whom I hear cheered on arrival to save the hero.

I wouldn't have recognized their footsteps had not Mr. Killingsworth declared so forthrightly to the Senate Assembly last month, while still editor, that he liked to think of The Daily as the "Conscience of the University"; that the paper would not accept any investigation of its editorial policies; that all kinds of things would be heard from afar if anyone should try.

If an officer trying to implement a moral rule is reprobate, and a concerned president is labelled sordid and a hypocrite (M. K., Feb. 26), from which source arises the indignation? From belief in a moral universe? From corporate conscience? They must differ deeply, of course, since one elicits Daily contempt, the other eternal protection. Yet under emergency both have been enforced by power. (The possee that came thundering down by telegram from Lansing proved fully as efficient as a police squad, no?)

Whence derives The Daily its justification for either morals or conscience, either private or public? And who is supposed to patrol this set of conscience watchers?

—*Kenneth L. Pike,*
Professor of Linguistics

Quarrels need two
For hate to mate.
I don't hate you.
Matthew 5:22, 25, 44; I John 3:15

"The tongue setteth on fire
the courses of nature."

(James 3:6)

"Recompense to no man evil
for evil."

(Romans 12:17)

Counting the Cost

Social action requires costly investment. Not only the scholar, but his wife also will be involved. She may resent this. She may feel too busy, or may prove unwilling to spend precious energy, needed for daily routine, on unappreciative others.

The man himself, on the other hand, will cringe — as we all do and as Christ did — when the moment of payment comes. Life comes only through death — of someone, something. The wheat abides alone, without death. The plants of earth die unless the sun dies. Only the eternal Father escapes this "thermo-dynamic" law.

"For which of you, intending to build a tower, sitteth not down first, and counteth the cost, whether he have sufficient to finish it?" (Luke 14:28).

Stifled Outreach

Why should I go
Beyond horizon mine
(Babe, clothes, man,
Demand attention's span) —
How find time?

These burdens grow,
Pound nerves to sand.
Serve my **neighbor's** child?
Don't talk wild.
More I can't stand.

Luke 10:40

Spend and Be Spent

"Love seeketh not her own" —
How else, give?
World grows by energy lost —
Else man abides alone.
Wheat seeks ground
For entropy to reverse.
Eternal Fire, Beyond,
Feeds life from Him.

**II Corinthians 12:15;
I Corinthians 13:5;
John 12:24**

CHANGE AND TRUTH

Students want security in the face of struggle — but where do they get it? And if they seem to get it now, can it last? Long? How about the passing of student generations? There is an attitude abroad among students that at the age of 30 life ends and stupidity begins. What is this change which comes with the passing of one generation and the reign of the next? And how does it affect truth itself? Does truth change with student graduation?

I was in a coffee shop some time ago with a professor who believes in cultural relativity. Finally he said, "I sometimes wonder if 30 years from now what I hold to be true people will hold to be false?" — since his own convictions of truth could not be expected to escape corrosion.

If cultural relativity is completely true, then belief in absolute cultural relativity must prove to be logically inconsistent and false.

So we talked. Finally he said that he always got gloomy thinking about it. He walked out.

> Security, where? —
> In **student** power?
> When age sneaks up,
> What holds then?
>
> In **cultural** norms,
> Our values clutched —
> No threat of loss
> By change?
>
> Pure,
> Unchanging,
> Always "there";
> God, our ever axiom.

(Students want security, and **some** kind of rightness. But whence? Based on what?)

Hebrews 11:6; 13:8

Stupidity Begins at Thirty

Age is bold:

> "Oaks from acorns grow,
> We're told."

Youth's crow:

> "You're old —
> How can **you** know?"

> (Youth feels that age uses empty —
> or false — clichés. Age feels
> that youth denies the obvious
> tested truth. What could be more
> accessible to sight by the aged
> than the growth of a tree? Or
> more unobvious to the very young?)

Truth in Person and His Word

Blind Pilate,
When Truth before him stood, said:
"What is truth?" — saw Him not.

Truth first
Finds source in person.
(From true Person flows true Word.)

Deaf Pilate,
While ears rang with Word "I Am,"
Heard Him not — no ear to hear.

John 18:37; 14:6; 17:3, 7, 14, 17

(As I see it, **unchanging** truth, and
ultimate absolute demands as to the
nature of personal character and morals,
are calibrated by the Person of Christ
and the nature of the Father. Matthew
5:48).

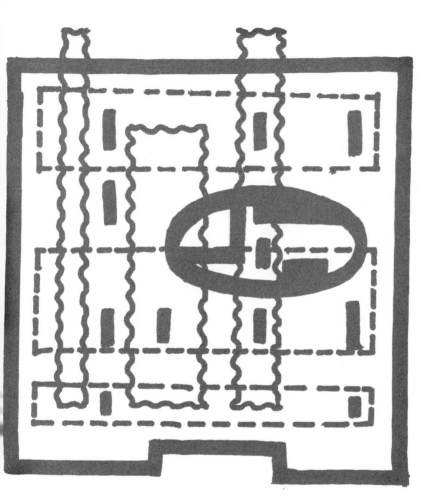

IV

THE SCHOLAR
and LANGUAGE

Human Computers

Most scholars must deal extensively with words. Language is for them a tool. By it they manipulate relationships, in mental "experiment" and "construction." Words are mental test tube and bulldozer. For the linguist like me, however, language plays a double role. Simultaneously it comprises the test tube and the solution. No wonder it fascinates! Man's **capacity** to speak a language is uniform. Or, to put it another way, the computer between man's ears is the "same model" from East to West, from North to South. Whether man is black, white, yellow, or brown, he has the same basic computer. This innate capacity is determined by birth. It is genetically carried and genetically limited.

On the other hand, we know that languages differ. Chinese is not English. How, then, can we say that language is in some sense genetically controlled? The answer has to be that language as a basic capacity is innate to the human species, but that a **particular** language comes from culture. To the linguist, man may appear like a computer in a closed room. The linguist, on the outside, wants to know how the computer is built, but the door is locked. The only thing he can see and study is the output. He can't see language with a surgeon's knife — nor does he know how to operate that way! But the output is not uniform, although there is but one computer in the room.

If the output comes out in sharply different forms, what controls the difference? It must be the different "programs." You can have a generalized computer, put a certain reel of tape onto it which feeds in instructions, and you can handle your accounts: $2 + 2 = 4$. Feed another reel to the same computer and it will print out addresses.

The human brain is like that. We all are built with one basic model, with capacities for learning and handling diverse programs — not only different languages, but, say, eating with chopsticks, or with knife and fork; we have the capacity to learn either way. That capacity works on the input from environment; but heredity and environment are relevant. Some years ago my daughter irritated me. She noticed that, and said, "Oh, Daddy, I'm so sorry. Do you suppose it is due to heredity — or to environment?" In either case, I was in trouble!

We are of one blood. The wheels whirl inside the computer and man can talk.

By working with an informant from a language new to us we can discover some of its particular characteristics. In Quechua it may be easy to tell noun roots from verbal ones; in Tagalog that may be difficult or impossible; English (what is "fish"?) may lie half way between. Certain characteristics of the universal computer, on the other hand, allow us to see languages from various perspectives.

We can view activity as a thing; for example, a person can even say, "I like beauty," as if beauty were something he could hold in his hand; or talk about time, or a race, as if they were not a process, but a thing. On the other hand, one can also talk about such an item as an experienced continuum, where events and even things merge and flow into one another, with special highlights. The event culminates in the most relevant — nuclear — part of the event, after which it tapers off. This gives a wave-like view of the world — and even a house can be seen from this second perspective. The construction phase is pre-nuclear, the new house is enjoyed at the peak of its life, and may then slowly decay to rubble. Houses are only occasionally thought of in this way — by historian, for example, or by nostalgic grandpa. A third perspective views elements as points in a network of relations — the house may be represented as a mere dot on a map which provides symbols for clusterings of houses but ignores differences between individual ones.

The human computer employs the same approach for all areas of human experience. Language capacity is one special instance derived from a more general capacity.

One of my contributions to linguistic theory has been an attempt to explore the implications of this view — of language as particle, as wave, and as field. Other characteristics of language are also more general than language itself. These must likewise be studied if we wish to know man. For example, we must be able also to recognize units, and tell one apart from another under changing circumstances. If I get engaged to a girl today, I need to be able to recognize her tomorrow. It would indeed be difficult otherwise. And yet, if she's had her hair done over, and put on a party dress, I might be startled at first sight. Yet I want to be able to identify this wonderful particle, and to tell her apart from others. We must, that is, be able to learn the contrastive and the identificational features of units, and be able to identify the various guises or disguises — variants — under which a unit appears in different contexts.

And then there is the relevance of distribution. Where does she appropriately appear? Where do we expect to find her? In what contexts? Appropriateness is a characteristic of the unit. A unit is well described, then, only if we know its contrastive features, its range of variability and the situations in which it normally occurs — including for persons as units their meaningful relationship to society, which provides them with roles as individuals.

All of this — and more — our computers must be able to master. And all the world is as competent — or incompetent — as we. No more; no less. King has no advantage at all over cannibal, here, in starting capacity.

OF ONE BLOOD

Wheels whirl,
Circuits flip:
Man talks —

Computerized
Communication's
Flesh and Blood.

Environment,
Heredity,
Interlock.

Genes draw but one
Circuit design
For all men.

Culture's tape
Feeds in the
Local Program.

Acts 17:26; Revelation 5:9

Our Tongue — A Rudder

Language has a peculiar power over us. It, in part, rules us. Our hearts, in part, rule it. This ambivalence is shown up in James 3:2-4, "For in many things we offend all. If any man offend not in word, the same is a perfect man, and able also to bridle the whole body. Behold, we put bits in horses' mouths, that they may obey us; and we turn about their whole body. Behold also the ships . . . are turned about with a very small helm." And "Doth a fountain send forth at the same place sweet water and bitter? Can a fig tree, my brethren, bear olive berries? or a vine, figs? so can no fountain yield both salt water and fresh" (James 3:11, 12). Out of the heart come words, often, unfortunately, hateful words. "The tongue can no man tame." We bless God with it, and curse man with it — we shouldn't do that. We know that our heart controls our words, we can't easily fake them.

On the other hand, the opposite side of this picture is that the words, to some degree, control the heart. "Even so the tongue is a little member, and boasteth great things. Behold, how great a matter a little fire kindleth! And the tongue is a fire, a world of iniquity; so is the tongue among our members, that it defileth the whole body, and setteth on fire the course of nature: and it is set on fire by hell."

The tongue, that is to say, is a rudder. Language has some kind of leadership in setting the psychological tone of the heart. I no longer dare to pretend (as I sometimes used to) that I'm unhappy — just for fun making believe that I'm grouchy — because again and again, within just a very short time, I have become grouchy. I've seldom been able, safely, to be sarcastic, because sometimes after it or with it has come the desire to hurt.

What then should we do? We can use this rudder positively. I have tried to, ever since my Dad said to me when I was a boy, "Why can't we study to say the kindly things for fun instead of the hurtful things?" A little encouragement may be **very** strengthening to someone else; we should try casting this happy bread upon the waters. By the grace of God we can use our tongues to help steer our psychology into happiness, joy, and courage.

Christ joyfully, deliberately, for the joy which was set before

Him, endured the cross (Hebrews 12:2). "By him therefore let us offer the sacrifice of praise to God continually, that is, the fruit of our lips giving thanks to His name" (Hebrews 13:15). Whether our emotions tell us that we **feel** like it or not, we should force ourselves to say, "Thank you."

When we say, "Thank you, Father," for that which is difficult; when we say, "Thank you, Father," when everything is dark, this is accepting God's way as good, even though it be an unwanted way (in some part of our being). Even as our Lord in Gethsemane said (cf. Matthew 26:39), "Not my will but thine" (i.e. "though in some sense I don't want it, let it go from me if possible; I accept it as of thy hand"). So we too are ready to be slain for the will of God; to accept the death of grouchiness.

What a comfort it is, I feel, sometimes to be grouchy! But my wife doesn't understand that. What is it in us that is so perverse? I don't know. Why do we delight to blame somebody else instead of acknowledging our own faults? Why do we delight in all kinds of things which are gloomy instead of enjoying the good grace of God over these? I don't know. I know only that overcoming it takes a sacrifice. "Though He slay me, yet will I trust Him" (Job 13:15). Kill these gloomy thoughts with thanksgiving to God in Jesus' name.

You see, saying "Thank you, Lord," for what I don't want, says that I accept God's unwanted way as being good. This also says that I trust the Lord. I can't say, "Thank you, Lord," for something I don't believe has come from Him — can I? So, it opens the door to trust, and thanksgiving opens the door for me to relax. If I say, "Thank you, Father," I know He's got all things under control.

The negative side of this — the refusal to force our tongues to say "Thank you, Lord" — is very sad, and ultimate ruin. You see this ruin in Romans 1:20. The "invisible" things are "seen" by everybody. The scholars were without excuse because, though they knew God was there, they didn't say "Thank you, Lord." When they refused to say this, the feedback on the soul led them to become proud. God was responsible for the good, but when they refused to say "Thank you" for the good, they **lost the ability to realize that God had sent the good.** The alternative was to believe that good came from some other place.

So they set up a different "model" to explain where the good came from. Refusing to have God in their knowledge, they attributed the good things of God to some other source. I saw some time ago this catastrophic chain at work in a lecture by one of my very famous (but older) contemporaries. He refused belief in God. When he looked around for another source of all things, he could suggest that physical things came from physical sources, from the mountains, or the molecules of the sea. But, it appeared to him, the good things of imaginative spirit must come from another who has it — it must come from man. This creative ability impressed him as greater than the mountains — therefore all the greatest good seemed to have its source in the understanding of man. And the greatest of this insight is from the smartest people (of which he **had** to be one, in order to figure this out). He was proclaiming, therefore, the divinity of man — with himself, by implication, at the top.

No wonder, caught in the midst of this chain, that the persons reported in Romans became proud in their imaginations and their foolish hearts were darkened. Professing themselves to be wise, they became, in fact, fools. But since something built into man does not allow his culture permanently to assume that he is God, he eventually has to transfer trust outside of himself. So they exchanged the glory of the incorruptible God for the likeness of four-footed beasts, and creeping crawling things. Nor was this the end of the chain. The next step was beastly corruption and immorality. It is no accident, therefore, that an incident like that involving defense of the obscene film Flaming Creatures (which I discussed in Chapter III) should occur on a highly **intellectual** campus.

What a letdown! And the rudder is the tongue — in part. And when scholars referred to in Romans refused to say "Thank you, Lord," they developed a trust — but not a trust in God. Instead they developed a trust in themselves, in a false philosophical base. This, it seems to me, is the result of their refusing to accept God as the basic axiom, and choosing — whether they wished to or not, by default — others which were inadequate. Then God gave them up to believe these false axioms (II Thessalonians 2:11). The product was every kind of moral stench.

*   *   *

If you give **Him** thanks, He'll give **you** joy. If you cease giving thanks, you'll soon cease to believe. If you cease to believe, you can't give Him thanks, and if you don't give Him thanks, He won't give you joy.

The tongue is a rudder; let's bend it to give thanks no matter how much it hurts. It hurts to kill our lugubrious gloominess. Let's give it up with joy and say, "Thanks." Let's give away the **right** to be gloomy — at least for today. Say "Thank you, Lord," for what we don't like, for we haven't chosen.

We can be especially grateful for some of these — because we know that if we were not responsible for them, they must come to us (ultimately) from the good hand of God — even if He has used evil hands to pass them on to us.

The Lord's Voice — and Ours

A linguistic element: "He that entereth in by the door is the Shepherd of the sheep. To him the porter openeth; and the sheep hear his voice; and he calleth his own sheep by name and leadeth them out. And when he putteth forth his own sheep, he goeth before them, and the sheep follow him: for they know his voice. And the stranger will they not follow, but will flee from him; for they know not the voice of strangers" (John 10:2-5).

Language is an extraordinary device. It indexes culture. It represents the personality structure. It identifies the individual. It is this identificational function which is so clearly and strikingly shown us here. We recognize a person by his voice. We follow because we hear his voice, and hearing his voice, we trust him because we know him.

Personality expresses what a man is, and his words allow this to come out so that it is recognizable by others. The Lord has the voice of a shepherd; he has the touch that is recognizable by sheep — stupid, wandering, jittery lambs. But they follow the voice, and in the long run every sheep will get to the fold. Not one will be lost, and not one will end up out of the way. They will end up in the fold, as they follow the voice.

In Revelation 3:19, 20, the pattern is picked up again: "As many as I love, I rebuke (with my voice) and chasten." "Behold, I stand at the door, and knock; if any man hear my voice, and open the door, I will come in to him, and will sup with him, and he with me."

In linguistics we have to deal both with the words and general character of the voice. While in Africa trying to see what the voice had to do with communication, I well remember working with an informant and one of my colleagues. If this informant were angry, he had breathy, rapid, powerful pronunciation — with lowered pitch, especially at the end of sentences. And along with this he would show his excitement by fast gestures and by rolling his wide-open eyes. If, however, he were talking to the Chief, and he wanted to show him respect, he would speak slowly, and quietly, with a slow nod of the head, and both hands rotated out flat. The voice identifies the man; the voice identifies the attitudes of the man — joy, sorrow, anger, fear, love (provided it is accompanied with the communicative gestures which go along with it).

Paul speaking at one time before a hostile audience said, "Men, brethren, and fathers, hear ye my defense which I make now unto you. And when they heard that he spake in the Hebrew tongue to them, they kept the more silence" (Acts 22:1, 2). The language in which a man was born has power to reach deep into the soul. One informant said to the translator, "I don't mind if that one scolds me in English, but you scold me in **my own language."**

A centurion was shaken by language (Acts 21:37 - 39). He had rescued Paul from a mob which would have torn him limb from limb, and as Paul was to be led into the castle for protection by the soldiers, he said unto the chief captain, "May I speak unto you, please?" who said, "Can you speak Greek? Aren't you one of the Egyptians we had trouble with last week? How do you speak Greek?" Paul said, "I am a Roman citizen, speaking Greek." And then he spoke in Hebrew, and he shook the audience, too. (Cf. Acts 21:37-38.)

I seem to recall that C. S. Lewis somewhere (I have not located the spot) told of a man saying to his wife, "Is breakfast ready yet?" — with a snarling tone of voice — and she threw the skillet at him. I've often wondered what would happen if they called him into court, with the judge, saying to him, "Tell me what happened?" Suppose he answered, "Well, I was just coming down for breakfast and I asked, 'Is breakfast ready yet?', and she threw the skillet at me." But he lied. He said, "Is breakfast ready yet" **plus** a snarling tone superimposed. It was the "plus" that got the skillet!

Voice identifies the attitude. Voice identifies the message. Voice identifies the man, his culture, his language, and his soul.

It isn't too surprising then that the Lord Jesus warns us about the use of our voice and our words. "A good man out of the good treasure of the heart brings forth good things: and an evil man out of the evil treasure brings forth evil things. But I say unto you, That every idle word that men shall speak, they shall give account thereof in the day of judgement" (Matthew 12:35, 36). Our words open up the veil and let our brothers know what we are; as we speak we calibrate ourselves. Unless a man is a powerfully competent hypocrite, his character will shine through his words fast.

But why the warning about idle words? Why can't I be judged by what I say when I'm on guard? Is it fair? Yes, it's fair. I fail by this test because, you see, when the **guard is down,** when the gate opens wide — for easy escape of heart's corruption, cursing, anger, sarcasm, or just plain lack of courtesy — **by our off-guard words our character is most especially revealed.**

Head Drunk

Wild chortle.
Liquid flows.
Loud blows.

Why Poetry?

Some time ago I had the opportunity to try, again, to learn to speak a new language. As a professional student of languages, I expected only the routine — but long and tedious — technical chores of vocabulary, grammar, pronunciation. I was in for a shock.

Once more — as if I had never tackled the job before since the time I grew up as a monolingual speaker of English in a town hostile to anyone found speaking any other language! — once more I felt deep cultural shock, a deep bitter nausea welling up as if to spew out in raging revolt all foreign customs, sounds, words which seemed to be invading to desecrate my very soul.

Language goes deep. It fuses with our personality structure (and our moral structure — is there any other way to say "ought"?). It grows up together. So a man brought up with just one language (the bilingual has far less trouble) is likely to feel the pressure to learn a new language as a subtle attack on himself.

This upset goes deeper than ordinary self-control can resist totally, and a kind of partial sickness may bother for a time. New missionaries, for such reasons, often need to be moved back to a rest post every six months or so, where they can hear English for a while and relax with "bread and butter" (instead of goat meat and tortillas, for example) and their own language.

Prose can tell us this — but often misses the feeling that goes with it. In order to tell my wife how I felt during this last struggle of mine (since she was not with me at the time) I wrote her a little poem called "Crushed" (which is given below). Poetry has special techniques, which sometimes allows a sustained grasp of emotional states difficult to duplicate in prose. The successful poem can then be read over and over, many times, leading one to relive the experience without decay.

Poetry differs from prose, although the line between the two is so vague as to leave specialists perplexed at definition. I like to think of the difference as one of linearly directed attention for prose,

$$\longrightarrow \quad \longrightarrow \quad \longrightarrow \quad \longrightarrow$$

as against multiple direction for poetry:

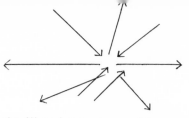

Scientific, expositional prose seeks (1) to have one word to one meaning, (2) in a logical, cumulative, linear sequence from one word to another. It is intended to be (3) unambiguous, so that no word says two things. It is to be (4) **non-redundant,** so that no element is stated twice.

Poetry, as I wish it to be, is ideally the opposite. (1) By using crucial words with multiple meanings (by pun, metaphor, or a variety of senses) a word can point backwards (to one idea) and forwards (to another) at the **same time;** this links the two. (2) The multiple connections achieved by these lexical devices (and others, such as the use of lexical sets like spring, summer, fall) are supplemented by phonological ones (where rhyme or stress may link words otherwise apart — e.g. **snow** and **flow).** (3) Grammatical balance (pointed out to me especially by Professor Roman Jacobson) may also serve this linking purpose (e.g. **haughty snow** linked with the **lava's flow).** Simultaneity, not sheer linearity, may be the goal.

By all these devices, multiple experience is elicited, to be relived by the reader. Since life itself is n-dimensional, some poetry — for some people — seems astonishingly closer to life than prose can be. Just as the child is not the scholar, but surpasses him in learning to speak the multiple dimensions of a new language, so poetry can mirror the n-dimensions of experience in a compact packet.

If the dry logical sequences of a scholar's expositional prose may be called non-redundant, then (I have suggested) this kind of poetic writing may be called **anti-redundant,** because of its n-dimensionality.

(The prose of a pedagogue — we now add to complete the set — is best when redundant. It carries planned redundancy, which repeats crucial lessons in various ways to help the memory.)

Except we become as little children, we can neither learn a new language without a bad accent, nor become charter citizens of heaven — nor experience that multiple fullness of the n-dimensional experience, which poetry tries to help us capture. Poetry compacts life in language — as an oak forces all its eternal blueprints into one nutshell.

108

CRUSHED

Through Culture strain
Where words like spears
Pierce rebel ear
Which screams with pain
Both dumb and blind.

(How **can** man love —
Or cope with woe —
Where systems wildly smash
Each others' proud unconscious plan?)

Our Father — to Whom
All speech is one,
And tongues of man
But image thin of Thine —
Help me now.

Luke 2:52; Phil. 2:7, 8;
Heb. 2:17; 5:8; Gen. 1:26;
Jn. 1:1.

(My language is a system of cast-
iron units, patterns, rules. So, precisely, is the language of — say —
Timbuktu. The clash between them
draws psychological sparks when I
try to shift from one set of whirling
gears to another. It hurts.)

It is time to repeat our commercial: Write to the Wycliffe Bible Translators, Box 1960, Santa Ana, California 92702, if you are interested in their Bible translation drive. For information about the academic courses, write The Summer Institute of Linguistics, Box 1960, Santa Ana, California 92702.

BREAKTHROUGH

My work as a linguistic consultant frequently takes me into situations of considerable and surprising complexity. There one sees that theoretical, linguistic, academic tools are sometimes very useful to help in solving the most practical of problems.

Not too long ago, in a workshop for the Summer Institute of Linguistics, Inc., and the Wycliffe Bible Translators, Inc., I was in Nigeria. There was an analytical problem with one of the languages of the area in which Miss Soutar of the Sudan Interior Mission was working. I would probably not be reporting the incident now, except it had been told by one of her mission colleagues, Mr. Harold Fuller, in the SIM official magazine, **Africa Now** (No. 31, Oct.-Dec. 1966), "The Sudan Interior Mission At Work." The rest of this essay is a direct quote from that source.

Linguists participating in the Linguistic Workshop held at the University of Nigeria, Nsukka, this year not only solved a complex Bible translation problem in neighboring Dahomey but also made a linguistic breakthrough which will affect translation around the world.

"This is a major step forward in the study of discourse," stated Dr. Kenneth L. Pike, a director of Wycliffe Bible Translators, who led the workshop.

The breakthrough came as the result of research done by Jean Soutar, SIM translator from Dahomey. Miss Soutar and her colleague Rosella Entz had found complex problems in revising a 1950 translation of the Gospel of John in Bariba.

The two Canadian missionaries had noticed that evangelists often changed the Scriptures to the third person when quoting. They would say, "Jesus said He is the way, the truth, and the life." When a missionary used the first person, "Jesus said, I am the way," the people responded, "All right, we shall follow **you**."

Changing the translation to fit the tribal use of third person narrative was not so simple, however. Illiterates didn't understand direct quotations; but nationals who had studied French (the official language) or who had trained under foreigners were accustomed to the first person form and said the third person form made the Scriptures too impersonal. Emotional feelings arose over the revision.

The missionaries wondered what to do. Translation came to a standstill. They prayed and continued research. Then a cable brought what proved to be the answer: SEND MISSIONARY TO LINGUISTIC WORKSHOP EXPENSES PAID.

The cable was the result of a visit to the SIM in Lagos, Nigeria, by Dr. Pike on his way to Nsukka. He reported that missionary linguists would be welcomed by the workshop sponsors. Over in Dahomey, the SIM District Superintendent decided Jean Soutar should go to Nsukka.

Consulting with Dr. Pike and other linguists at the workshop, Miss Soutar once again went through the recorded conversations in fables and tribal history she and Miss Entz had collected. As she classified the material, she prayed. Then suddenly Jean knew she had found clues to a solution.

A pattern began to take shape — so intricate that it had been missed before. In recounting a tribal fable around his compound fire, an elder used indirect quotes (third person) in his introduction. This the linguists labelled "off stage." When he got to the action part, he changed to direct quotes (first person) — "on stage."

"Focus" was another factor in determining which form to use: the way attention was focused on the action or on the conversation itself. This became further complicated when one character used third person and another used first person. Explanation: the "focus" of the story was on the hero, not the villain! The choice of first or third person was also governed by who was speaking and to whom he was speaking.

It was complicated, but there **was** a pattern! It wasn't a question of using only third person or only first person. Both had to be used, according to a complex system of action, focus, and other factors. No wonder people had disagreed about the Bible translation, no matter which way it had been done!

Dr. Pike was as excited as Jean Soutar when she explained what she had found. Together they worked out a formula for applying the pattern to newly written languages. Languages in other parts of the world have similar patterns, but until now translators have not used such a formula for discourse. The Bariba discovery would help translators around the world — "a major step forward," in Dr. Pike's opinion.

112

Jean Soutar is now back in Dahomey with her colleague Rosella Entz, testing the technique on Bariba readers. Finding the pattern and constructing a formula were important, but only the beginning of a formidable task. Now they have to apply these to every quotation in Scripture.

For instance, they will have to decide which is correct in Bariba:

(1) Jesus said, "No one can come to the Father but through Me"; or

(2) Jesus said that no one can go to the Father but through Him.

Whether a quarter of a million Baribas will one day be able to **understand** the Scriptures in their own language will depend on many such linguistic decisions.

Concentration

There is something extraordinary about life and time. They are not uniform. They do not seem to proceed steadily. There are times and seasons when life's events merge in immense concentration.

Language — especially anti-redundant poetry — can portray such moments and help us to grasp them. It can also take vast spans of history and bring them together in a compact report. A history of the Middle Ages is like a language telescope. By it we can **see** the extended whole, the forest for the trees. Drama is like that, too. In a two-hour play a generation of tragedy may be lived — and **felt**. Deep calls to deep. Language is its trumpet.

I Lived a Year in Three Short Weeks

Stars own their telescopes
Through which the eye
Stares at their focused gleam.

Words amass the glow
Of spoken petals
Like perfume torn from rose.

And I — have lived compressed
Both time and joy,
A year, just weeks ago.

NO EMPTY UNIVERSE

Some scholars are curiously uninformed about Biblical Christianity. They think that Christians are so egocentric that they think that the whole universe contains only man-plus-God (who in turn exists for man). But, these scholars argue, if we **really** understood the laws of probability we would see that it is overwhelmingly certain that there **must** be other galaxies like this one, other planets like this one, therefore concatenations of forces which led to atoms, heavy proteins, and living organisms, and even creatures comparable to those of earth. How stupid we must be, they imply — how egocentric — to assume that we alone are sentient in this vast world of the stars!

It interests me, on the other hand, to note the man-tied imagination of many writers of science fiction. Often, when trying to create weird imaginary beings the best they can do is to suggest a metal manlike Martian with antennae sticking out of its cranium. This represents only a very small change from ears — merely receptors for waves known to us. There is really no basic difference.

Few people that I meet, however, seem to have been curious enough to think seriously about the most extraordinary beings (just one kind among many) which Christianity or Judaism mentions — the seraphim. Six wings (Isaiah 6:2). "With twain he covered his face." I wonder why? As a symbol of the holiness of God? "With twain he covered his feet." Why? As a symbol of modesty? And with two of them, only, he flew — through what kind of air?

In Ezekiel, the first chapter, there is a further extraordinary set of creatures. Out of the midst of the brightness, out of the fire, out of this major energy source (as if there were a birthplace of atomic might right there) came four creatures. They had the likeness of a man. Four faces. Why? I have no idea — although various people have proposed speculative answers to such questions. Four wings. Why? And their feet were straight feet, like the sole of a calf's foot. They sparkled. They had the hands of a man under their wings, and faces in their wings. They didn't turn when they went. Is this why they had wings on all sides? Their four faces were different. One was like a man. One was like a lion. One like an ox, and one like an eagle. (If this is by chance a simple metaphor, **what** is it a metaphor **of?**)

They went straight forward. They didn't turn as they went. Were these "creatures"? They ran. They returned. And their appearance was like a flash of lightning. You couldn't see them, they were so fast. (I wonder if they went faster than the speed of light. I don't see how God can control things unless He can act fantastically faster than the speed of light. How would He ever catch up to a star? Or an angel? The speed of light must be a limiting factor of our world culture — it can have nothing whatever to do with limits on God.) And the creatures had "wheels." They were curious wheels; they didn't go round and round. They are hierarchically ordered — wheels within wheels. They had eyes round about. They could see in any direction without turning. Is this metaphor?

117

To me as linguist, two points are of special interest. Where the spirit of the creatures wants to go, they go. Is that thought control? Teleportation? In addition, there was a lot of noise around them. Did they have their loudspeakers on — for communication signals the author could neither recognize nor translate? Some of the Scriptural creatures were obviously able to interact with the communication devices of our culture. There was the angel who went up before the parents of Samson in a flame of fire (Judges 13). Gabriel was able to recognize Mary's fear (Luke 1:30).

What I am trying to point out is that the Scriptures, whether taken in full literalness or in metaphor, by no means allow belief in an empty universe.

Does the universe look the same from an "angel's-eye view," from the perspective of a sinless creature in God's presence? Apparently not. In I Peter 1:12 one of the most extraordinary Scriptures is found. It refers to these heavenly powers and says that unto them "it was revealed that not unto themselves, but unto us they did minister the things, which are now reported unto you by them that have preached the gospel unto you with the Holy Ghost sent down from heaven" — that is, the Gospel and the cross — "which things the angels desire to look into." Perhaps, if they don't themselves need redemption, these creatures want to study **us,** as in a play (I Corinthians 4:9), to see about the cross.

Egocentricity is scientifically unavoidable. No science can operate, no mathematical formula serve, without a starting point where the observer takes his real or his pretended stand. Language cannot operate without **some** bench mark in reference to which it can retain coherent orientation as it surveys the scene. Nor can man, whether physicist or theologian. It is the nontheist — not the inheritors of the Judeo-Christian tradition — who elevates the useful but arbitrary humanity bench mark into the status of eternal psychological center, when he makes man — instead of the person of God — the absolute measure of all things meaningful and moral.

As linguist, also, I speculate on the kind of **lingua franca** which some day in heaven will link us all — human, non-human, seraphim, and God — in one communication network, but with roots of our past, and every tongue (cf. Revelation 5:9) contributing to the preservation of our identity and individuality.

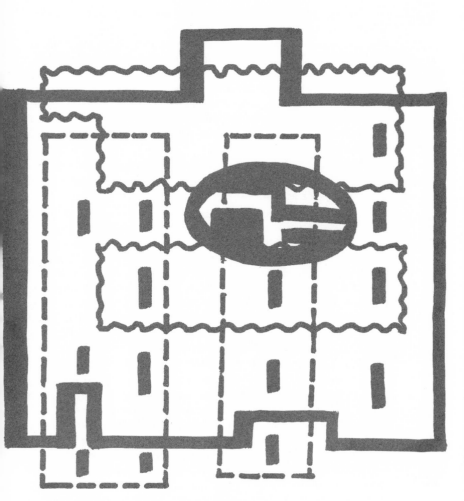

V

THE SCHOLAR
and COMMITMENT

EVER-FLOWING SPRING

120

I was brought up in Connecticut, in a little country community which didn't amount to anything. It was not even a crossroads, just half of one! Our grocery store doubled for everything — post office, hardware store, dry goods. Dad was the physician in town, right in the center across from the New England common. The common is still there, although they don't herd the cows on it the way they used to in the early days when they set up the common.

Dad joined with a group of a half dozen families who had a kind of neighborhood co-operative to get water to their houses. A glacier had come down thousands of years before and with giant claws had scratched out rock and debris between two hills, leaving a little valley. In that valley was a little spring, half a mile up the way. There was a pipe about as big as my thumb, which brought the water down the valley to our houses. Under the old squeaky pitcher pump in the kitchen was a barrel where the water was stored safe from the frost of the cold New England winter, which sometimes froze the ground — enough to break pipes — three feet deep. We were allowed a stream of water about as big as the lead of a lead pencil to squirt from an off-shoot of the main line into the barrel. (If you took more and cut the pressure for houses farther up the hill, there was trouble.) Because of this ever-flowing spring, there was always pure, clear water in our barrel. It was always there to pump, always overflowing, unless we drew it out in tubs for our Saturday night bath.

In 2 Samuel we are told about the time when David was hot and tired and remembered the cool refreshing spring water. "Oh, how good a cup of water would taste," he thought. So he sent three important men — important in the days when one man could put 10,000 to flight — to fetch some water. They slashed through the mob to get a cup of water for their king.

"You asked for water, here it is," they said as they returned.

When David took that precious cup he said, "More is in this cup than water. In it is the life of my men, men important to the kingdom. I cannot drink it selfishly."

The scholar, as mighty man, must break through language barriers to bring the water of life to people who do not have the Bible in their own language. It will, of course, entail risk — to the man, to his family, to his colleagues.

The Three Mighty Men

brake through the host of the Philistines, and drew water out of the well of Bethlehem, that was by the gate, and took it, and brought it to David: nevertheless he would not drink thereof, but poured it out unto the Lord.

And he said, Be it far from me, O Lord, that I should do this:

Is not this the blood of the men that went in jeopardy of their lives?

II Samuel 23:16, 17

WATER

Water. To the least (or
Last) — one cool cup
Reaches Him. Then
Who receives the
Barrel, full overflowing, the
Word (articulate
Life Itself) for thirst?
What precious gift to
King, from pool, by
David's Mighty Men!
"So send I you. Go."

Mark 9:41; John 4:14, 17, 18;
II Samuel 23:15

(This poem is written from the standpoint of God, who
sends us. Presently — in Preliterate Tribe — we write as
from the viewpoint of a tribesman. Later — in Committee
Meeting on Strategy — we take the stand of a group of
missionaries discussing plans and guidance.)

Focus on Tribes

God has new movements for new times, and new people for new jobs. When we try to say how, or where, the details may be blurred. But the fact that many students are becoming increasingly interested in Bible translation for tribal groups allows us to suggest that part of the will of God is that His Word get to the ends of the earth now — and quickly.

In New Guinea several years ago I was helping on twenty languages as consultant to my junior colleagues. While I was there a jeepload of us went out to visit a village of the Kanite tribe. It is a dull, colorless village with thatched huts and dirt-smeared bodies. The people there have — from our perspective — a drab existence. Their music, for example, is made on a little piece of bamboo with which they make a "twang twang" noise for hours on end, or on a little flute with which they play the same few notes over and over.

As I left, the translator in that tribe was talking to some of the people. A little old lady was explaining to her (the others tried to shush her up, but the little old lady didn't shush) that when a woman dies her children have to pay the neighbors to eat her up. When a sister dies, her brother can eat her if he paid for the privilege while she was still alive. In some of the nearby tribes, when some of the old men die, the way to get part of their strength is to put them on a platform, collect the drip a few weeks later, and then drink it. Cannibalism is, of course, illegal, but in areas opened up to civilization and governmental control only within the last few decades, habits do not disappear overnight.

Now what can we do in a place like that? The answer — we can give them the Word of God. It can give them courage in troublous times, ease their movement into the twentieth century, and point the way to new life. But the task seems so hopeless! How can we reach 2,000 and more tribes, people in the backwash of civilization?

They are small, anyway. Who notices **them?** In the past, few people, indeed — an occasional missionary, or trader, or government commission. But two circumstances change the picture. On the one hand, exploding population is pushing into frontier areas where few men went before. This easily opens the door to damage by unscrupulous men who want the land for planting or the wild products for trade — and sometimes take both at the expense of sparse tribesmen, if government is not watchfully preventing it.

On the other hand, many tribes — even large ones — have for years been ignored by governments of underdeveloped countries which have been in desperate struggle to increase their gross natural product, to build an industrial base, to bring schooling to the unbirthcontrolled masses. Some of these tribes, however, have suddenly been thrust into national and even international focus. Whereas previously they appeared to contribute neither good nor ill to the nation, and were left to their poor hillsides or swamps, they may suddenly receive promises of future wealth and knowledge along with immediate arms and ammunition from rebel sources which threaten the nation. In this case, the national interest may turn the spotlight on them, attempt at long last a crash program of education, community health services, and economic aid.

In this sense, as we also work for them to give them God's Word, we are with their governments on the forward wave of history, the history which God makes. We can see His hand in this, bringing His tribes into focus. We in linguistics are on His front lines. For the task of reaching these tribes with God's Word we are not left helpless or hopeless. Fifty years ago it was, perhaps, hopeless, and so they were often ignored. But this is no longer true. God has given us tools and techniques commensurate with this tremendous, otherwise hopeless task. These tools include the science of linguistics.

In the Mazatec language of Mexico, "father," "devil," and "Lord" are pronounced almost the same. And in Cakchiquel of Guatemala "our Saviour" and "a deceiver" are almost alike. If you mix these words up, how are the Mazatecs and the Cakchiquels going to know what you are saying? It's easy to make blunders, but today, with scientific linguistics, it isn't necessary to make blunders for long.

Fifty years ago it took a genius, more or less, to do a good translation job. It doesn't any more. In missions, that is big news for the twentieth century. Ordinary people are now doing a job which just a few years ago would have been acceptable as a dissertation.

The ordinary man can carry on the job because he is a member of a team. This team includes specialists in linguistics, as consultants to the other members of the team. We need the scholar, then, for without him the team doesn't do its job.

It is God, in the last analysis, who has turned our focus to the tribes. He has always been concerned. But the hour has come.

LOOK!

"Without My Father"?

Yes yes, I know
Masses of men, stars, warriors
Llaman la atención. But
When by one lone
Flea I'm bit,
I scratch. What calls forth
My focused eye — or God's?
Ninety-nine? One sparrow exiled
From world and heaven's flocks?

Luke 9:13, 25; 15:4-7

PRELITERATE TRIBE

I'm small,
Ignored —
No gun, bomb,
Pen, or tongue
To politic the world.

Weep for me!
No choice to grow —
Where's MY identity?
You have yours —
    Or smash your world
    To claim it . . .

    I'm just
    Not seen
    By mass of men
    IMPORTANT
    In **their** eyes.
But God's? —
    The widow's mite?
    The 99th plus
    one?

I'll live by Him —
Not culture's baksheesh.
I count as man,
Not beast.

With groans unutterable
    He weeps for me,
    Lazarus, bound
In wordless tomb
By culture's shroud.

John 11:33, 35, 38, 44

127

Spiritual Styles

The will of God is never identical for all men seeking identical goals. God's will, like white light with its multitude of diverse components, disperses into a spectrum of action channels as it works itself out through different personality structures.

Ezra was ashamed to ask for soldiers to protect his expedition — he had boasted that God would care for all who seek Him. But Nehemiah presumably accepted soldier escort. Both were going to rebuild in Jerusalem.

When Ezra wished to protest against a rash of mixed marriages — someone recently pointed out to me — he pulled out the hair of his own beard, and shamed people into repentance. When Nehemiah tackled the same problem, he yanked out the hairs of the offenders' beards (Ezra 8:22; 9:3; Nehemiah 2:9, 13, 25).

Initiative and guidance come from many different sources, all "spiritual" in that they please God when rightly used. In one tiny section of Ezra (7:15-18) an extraordinary range is seen. Upon observing a gap in needed roles — lack of priestly Levites — he knew (by **judgment)** that they should be sought — so he worked at it. He sent for certain men of **insight.** These then came, and were sent on a journey by guidance or initiative at **second hand,** i.e., through Ezra's instructions. These then went to Iddo, a leader, with Ezra's message. Iddo, in turn, found the **general** will of God in the request of Ezra — coupled, presumably, with the insightful report of his messengers. Iddo and the messengers, in turn, selected folk to go — whose guidance was the urging and judgment or **orders** of their leader Iddo, plus the persuasive insight of the messengers. Among those carefully selected was a man of **discretion** — who presumably would use that discretion in such a way that it would become a component in the guidance of others by — ultimately — God.

Too often, in discussing guidance, we think only of Paul's special conversion, or of the revelation to initial leaders. What would happen in the office of a mission board, or of a church, or of a bank if every stenographer waited extensively every time to get God's direct guidance before consenting to type or mail a check to someone desperately in need?

Differences of spiritual style, however, sometimes extend to different emphases within God's work as a whole. Leaders differ as to their outlook, plans, goals, enthusiasms, and initiative. Differences should be viewed with charity, and seen as evidence of God's varied interest — not as proof of human blindness or folly.

Committee Meeting on Strategy

Jerusalem?
    "Aye."
Cities?
    "Of course! (Paul Did.)"
Scattered fragments?
    "I move to delete* 'to the uttermost parts.'
    We're busy — and too important."

*Later, Christopher Magellan moved to substitute "postpone" for "delete" — as being "more accurate." This caused considerable debate.

(God wishes to reach the whole range of human needs— of all kinds of peoples. Seldom does any one mission or man feel with equal intensity the needs — of all kinds of peoples. Seldom does any and be efficient. Here, by implication, I intend to show my own strong feeling that tiny tribal groups must not be left out of the total planning.)

Surprise in Role Specialization

What intellectual, after conversion to Christianity, was the one who above all desired to reach the intellectuals of Jerusalem? It was Paul, the outstanding young man of promise. He had been their bright light, the leader of the future.

Paul was, therefore, the obvious man to reach the scholars with whom he had worked and studied. He felt this responsibility deeply, so he wanted to go to Jerusalem and to do something about it. But (cf. Acts 22:18) Paul heard his Lord saying, "Hurry up, get out of Jerusalem. They won't listen to you." But Paul argued: "Look, I was responsible for persecuting people in this city. I was involved in the Sanhedrin. These are people to whom I should witness. **I am the logical man. It ought to be my role.**"

The Lord replied to Paul, "No. It cannot be your role. They won't listen, even if scholar ought to listen to scholar. Get out — I'm sending you somewhere else."

So he went to the people of Asia Minor. Eventually he contacted the intellectuals of Athens; these — again his logical audience — did not respond. He got depressed and left to work with the non-intellectuals of Corinth.

Strangely enough it was the equivalent of a hillbilly, a practically uneducated fisherman from the "backwoods" province of Galilee, who was destined to reach those of Jerusalem — those who could be reached at all. When Peter was with Jesus at the time of His trial, scoffers said to him, "Your speech labels you — you are one of those backwoods fishermen from Galilee." A man from a low-class dialect, a low-prestige area, teamed up with low-status people to upset the intellectuals of his culture!

We seldom think of the area that Christ chose to come to as being itself of low status. We seldom stop to remember that he chose a small tribe, Judah, from an inconspicuous, weak nation. The intellectuals of Greece, of Rome, of Egypt, of Mesopotamia — these he left to one side. He came to a small group of tribesmen in an unimportant country, rather than to one of the highly civilized cities of the west — or the masses of the Orient. This particular priority placed on a small area, on the lost sheep of the house of Israel, surprises us — but God had other men in mind for the later role of outreach to the masses.

In Galatians 2:9 the idea of role specialization becomes very explicit. There was a fuss because some were saying that Paul should work as others did. Paul answered, "No, I have my own ways of working. These were given to me specially, and I must follow them. This does not destroy somebody else's role, nor can I allow someone else to force my role to his. We complement each other."

In the will of God there is **not just one pattern.** There are varied roles in the body of Christ. Let's seek God's role for us, and then set our faces like a flint, as Jesus did, to fulfill that. And let's not be surprised if it differs from what we early guessed it would be. Paul's role was vastly different from what he would have chosen for himself.

To all of us it proves somewhat frightening to **choose** a role. We would prefer to have God choose it for us, as He did for Paul. Yet for many — perhaps the majority — the choice is to accept a call in the style of Timothy or Silas — i.e., stimulated by the vision of another. This comprises a different spiritual style of guidance.

In it, of course, there lies risk. One can be wrong, the leader may himself have been deluded — or bumbling. Here trust in God must include belief in His gentleness and mercy even in our errors. It must also include the belief that He wants spiritual initiative, working out in social action — and repudiate the totally passive man who refuses to take a risk.

That, at least, is the lesson I read in the parable of the talents (Matthew 25:25-26). **Whatever** we choose will be O.K. — "prosper" is the Scriptural term — if we meet the spiritual conditions. (1) Not take basic advice from evil sources; (2) Not have evil as bosom friend; (3) Not tear down (as useless social action) instead of building; (4) Bend the tongue to rejoice, for its rudder effect and its righteousness; (5) Stick close to the Bible for principles of action, morals, and faith (Psalm 1).

Do this first. Then **take the risk.** And relax.

No Happy Life Lacks Risk

Spice:

    Cinnamon on cabbage;

Salt:

    'Of the earth' — or potatoes.

Blah:

    Futile words, empty act;

Boredom:

    Job, strife, or aimless Ph. D.

Risk:

    Trace-ingredient as spice of joy;

Faith:

    The cosmic salty

Choice.

Luke 19:20; Hebrews 11:15-16.

'I do not think the forest would be so bright, nor the water so warm, nor love so sweet, if there were no danger in the lakes.' (Hyoi to Ransom, in OUT OF THE SILENT PLANET, by C. S. Lewis.)

My blue refrigerator
Stands in spotless corner
Matched by towels and sink.

*　　　*　　　*

— Now let's think.

*　　　*　　　*

Both bugs and dirt
'll soil rug (?) and skirt,
'n my esthetics'll hurt.

I'd build bridge to heaven
With trestle of sweat
(And cultural blunders, I bet).
Money'd go blow —
Don't I know peace corps
Or missions'd leave me sore

Wounded in purse (or, worse, hearse)? and
Override materialism, and
Two-eyed blearialism?
How on foot or earth
Could I climb mountain ridge,
Or exchange fridge for — Bridge?

*　　　*　　　*

Serve in Viet?
Nyet. Not yet.
(= Go? No.)
I'LL SURE PRAY
(But stay if I may.
Hip Hurray!).

Matthew 6: 19-21; 19: 22, 23, 29-30;
Mark 10: 22; Acts 5: 1-11

The alternative — if one refuses the risk of loss in
service — is often the attempt to cling to material
possessions — sometimes with surface rationali-
zation of the deeper reason.

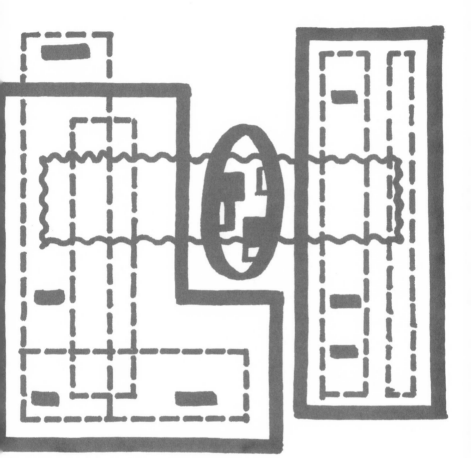

VI

THE SCHOLAR
AS TRANSLATOR

How I Fared . . .

In previous essays I have implied that a scholar should on occasion leave his ivory tower.

I tried it, for God and His Kingdom. Here is a brief, spotty record of that experience. I chose to work with a tribe of American Indians, high in the mountains (8,000 feet) of southern Mexico, called the Mixtecs. The tribe as a whole numbered about 200,000, half of whom spoke some Spanish — but I knew none whatever, and the director-founder of the work, Dr. William Cameron Townsend, wanted me to stay that way for a while until I had learned enough Mixtec to be sure it would continue to be more familiar to me than Spanish-as-potential-crutch.

How well I can relive the day when, swinging my skinny legs over the side of a donkey, I zigzagged up, up from the dry valley, from the train station at Parian, in the State of Oaxaca.

The snapping crack of the whip by the driver of the burro train, the zigzag trail too steep to run straight, the whistling doll train soon far below on its narrow gauge in the gorge — all these still make me catch my breath, as I write. Memory's sharp lines feel like a poem begging me to write it to store the glory of that hour in deep freeze for old age dessert.

This I said to my little burro with youth's exultation, "This indeed is being a missionary," and for four days I rode—or walked — onward to the Mixtec heights of hill, wounds, tone, or pain.

Most of that story must remain unwritten. Here, however, I back up a few months from that trip, to preparation for it in Mexico City.

MIXTEC BEGINNINGS — 1935

Before I had left Mexico City for the Mixtec area, Mr. Townsend had found a Mixtec language informant to give me a little advance start before going to the tribal area. He was an old colonel who had served in the Revolutionary Army. Since I knew no Spanish, Mr. Townsend said he himself would be with me an hour or so, to get me under way. I would then be on my own with the monolingual approach. That is, I would then have to learn the language like a baby — by living immersed in it. By gesture, pointing to this or that without an interpreter. O. K. — he wanted me to be a guinea pig to try out the idea; I was happy to try. (Some readers who know me well will recognize this as a source of the monolingual demonstration, which I use now to show students how to do the same thing in emergency; it has certainly paid off.)

We arrived at the one-room home where the old man and his wife lived. Townsend introduced me, we chatted a while, then left. Outside the house Townsend said to me, "Kenneth, next time don't show your disappointment so keenly."

I was, I admit, a bit disappointed, even down in the mouth. I had had only ten days of training in phonetics, and already felt incompetent enough. But this old man **didn't have any teeth!** **How** can you study the phonetics of a language if your informant doesn't have teeth? His "s" sounds blur. Tongue tip doesn't place itself right.

I figured I could survive that; but there was another problem. The old man was an invalid and **couldn't get out of bed.** In the monolingual approach when you can't jump, stand, run, walk, or find bugs and trees to point at, how do you get words to write down?

These two hurdles were a bit overwhelming, but there was another problem that made them pale in comparison: the man was **totally blind!** . . . So, my young reader, if you ever have a day in the tribe when you think your language informant troubles are bad, just remember — next time, please don't show your disappointment so keenly. It's just not done. Ho hum. I was learning more than language.

Finally, after a trip which took several days — over a 10,000-foot pass — I reached the area of the Mixtecs and started more vigorously to learn the language. Christmas was coming in a few weeks, and I was in a hurry to get the Gospel out. I wanted to translate the Christmas Story.

For that I needed the word for sheep, and the expression for John the Baptist. But I had difficulty interpreting the gestures the Mixtecs made for sheep. It was very confusing. It turned out that a high-pitched "baa" mimicked a goat — not a lamb — whereas a low-pitched one meant a sheep! I also tried in those early weeks to get the word for baptize. I had been told a story about some baby skunk needing to be baptized; its parents were looking for a godfather for the babe. They approached a lion — who wasn't particularly delighted to be the godfather to a skunk. Anyhow, they baptized the skunk. Then as I worked on the Christmas Story I tried to get the facts concerning John the Baptist, still, of course, using my monolingual approach, but taking an occasional peek at a dictionary for a troublesome word here and there. It wasn't long before I realized that I'd taken too big a chunk for the word "baptized." I had John going out into the wilderness to baptize — **skunks.**

I struggled hard to learn the language, but my ten days of phonetics training were not enough to help me solve the tone problems — a total of only ten minutes of class time was devoted to tone in those days. A year after I had started working, one of the Mixtec fellows said to me, "Pike, do you know why I didn't keep on working for you last year?" I said, "No." He said, "You promised that you would pay me so much for working ə̄ə̀ hours, but what you meant was that you'd pay me that much for working ə̄ə̄ hours." I finally found out that ə̄ə̀ is "nine" and ə̄ə̄ is "one." (The pitch of the voice falls on "nine," but is level on "one.") I was paying him a satisfactory hourly wage, but he became suspicious because I said I was paying him only that much money for nine hours. Nevertheless, off and on I kept saying, "This language can't be tonal because it keeps changing all over the place. Sometimes one is ə̄ə̄ and sometimes it's ə́ə̄." Nine sometimes was ə̄ə̀ and sometimes ə́ə̀. (Both words sometimes start higher than usual before the pitch falls. "Morphophonemics" is the technical name for this phenomenon.) I didn't know that tones could change and have different phonetic shapes in different contexts.

I was embarrassed. By now — another year later — I was supposed to be teaching phonetics at the small training course of the Summer Institute of Linguistics, but I didn't have the answers to tone problems in my own language. Other colleagues were coming down to Mexico to work and were meeting further tonal languages in the State of Oaxaca. My sister Eunice was one of them. I was the 'old man' of the outfit and was supposed to have the answers, but didn't. I was responsible; but I myself had problems.

Why Bother?

"Have not two, ten, or fifty,
tried in vain
to serve
Repulsed —
or lost midst bugs,
disease, revolt,
or stares?
Let them die."

(Of course one can give up
the whole idea of service.
Initial glow fades.
But the price —
to be paid by others —
will be high.)

PERSUADED TO WRITE — 1936

A year after the beginning, I found myself, with a broken leg, in a hospital. After a thirty-two hour wait and trip to get there, I had my leg in a basket since it was too late to put it safely in a cast, and with a fever of 101 from malaria which had broken out with the shock of the broken leg. There I was in the hospital—writing phonetics.

This part of the story is told by Ethel Wallis (from **Two Thousand Tongues to Go,** Harper and Row, 1960):

*　　　*　　　*

In the fall of 1936 after he had finished his first season of teaching phonetics, Pike helped his sister and Florence Hansen get settled in a clammy cold Mazatec village separated from his Mixtec town by several days through rugged mountains. By speaking the little Spanish which he by then had picked up, he rented quarters for the girls in a Mazatec house where they could begin their language work. He helped them to extract the first words from co-operative informants, with further instructions on how to start writing the unanalyzed Mazatec language.

Very early in the language lessons they discovered a pair of words that sounded exactly alike, except for the musical tone of the second syllable. That was the only difference in the words for "shirt" and "pig."

"Watch that tone," warned Pike. "It makes a difference, a difference in the meaning of words." But he hadn't figured out just what difference tone made in his own Mixtec language. He warned them anyway.

Leaving the first two Wycliffe women pioneers on their own to struggle with tone tangles and strange Indian food, Pike made his way down the mountain to the train station where he would take off for his Mixtec country. While waiting for the train, he lent a hand to some Mexican laborers who were unloading bags of grain from the freight cars at Parian—his jumping-off place on the railroad. Losing his balance under the weight of one of the loads, Pike slipped and broke his leg. Through the help of kind Mexicans he managed to arrive at the Baptist hospital in the city of Puebla where he received first-class medical treatment. His leg was put in traction, and he was safely settled in a clean white hospital bed.

Pike had been impatient to get back to his tribe in the Oaxaca mountains. He was eager to begin a second round with the elusive tone he had not yet conquered. He could hardly wait, but now he had to. It would take a while for the leg to mend.

"I wonder why this had to happen?" was the natural question he frequently asked during the first long hours. "What have I done which has displeased the Lord?" But as far as Pike could find his spiritual house was in order. "What **haven't** I done that I should have done?" He began to take another inventory.

There was one thing he hadn't done. He hadn't followed Uncle Cam Townsend's suggestion about **writing** something on phonetics. And he really hadn't wanted to. He was eager to learn the Mixtec language and to translate the Scriptures for the Mixtec people, but he wasn't thrilled at the thought of other writing. Townsend had not been trained linguistically before he went to Guatemala and translated the Cakchiquel New Testament. "He worked it out by the sweat of his brow in prayer and pain as he tore the language apart." Now he was seeking a way to make it easier for other translators and he knew that Pike could help.

As he woke up the next day in the hospital Pike decided to follow the request of his leader. Propping his paper on a book before him in bed he began to write phonetic symbols with explanations of them in English. It was difficult at first, but he wrote. He forced himself to write eight hours a day for about three weeks until convalescence demanded all his strength. He could make the sounds, but it was hard to describe them and to make explanations about the system of which they formed a part.

Finally he produced a one hundred and twenty-five page manuscript.

Within a few weeks after this assignment was finished, Pike's leg mended sufficiently for him to hike the rugged trail back to the Mixtec Indians.

Townsend had had correspondence with Professor Edward Sapir, one of the pioneers of descriptive linguistics in the United States, who was scheduled to teach at the University of Michigan in the summer of 1937.

Townsend felt Pike should therefore go to Michigan, and accordingly made the necessary arrangements. Pike arrived on the campus the last day of registration. He made his way toward the office of Dr. Charles Fries, the professor at Michigan at whose initiative the Linguistic Institute had been brought to the school and who invited Dr. Edward Sapir to give the special summer courses in descriptive linguistics.

In his office Dr. Fries had just hung up the receiver. It was a message from Western Union stating that an emergency would prevent one of the applicants from attending the session. His scholarship was canceled.

"Then there was a knock at the door," Dr. Fries recounts, "and there stood Kenneth. He had arrived without a scholarship, but here was one for him."

Ken Pike spent a very profitable summer with Dr. Sapir. And it was through working with him that Pike got a clue which eventually helped him to crack the Mixtec tone puzzle. He had been concentrating on the individual Mixtec words that caused trouble, but Sapir said that pitch, or tone, in language was "a matter of relationships — the pitch of each word should be compared with the pitch of others." With this hint Pike later developed an attack on tone languages helpful to linguists around the world.

Both Fries and Sapir saw the linguistic possibilities of the young missionary, but Pike himself had not yet seen the potentialities of linguistic study. His mind was on Mixtec. He wanted to learn just enough to do a good job of translating the New Testament for a needy tribe.

At the end of the course, "we talked about his going on," said Dr. Fries. "He didn't seem very much interested. He was such an able person that I thought it was a shame that he didn't go on and develop so that he really could make a satisfactory contribution. He showed great ability."

The following summer Pike was back at Michigan for further research. He was invited to address the Linguistic Institute. According to the report of the discourse appearing in the **Michigan Daily** on July 15, 1938, Pike included in it more than pure linguistic information:

"Sleeping on an earth floor, attended by the enthusiastic ministrations of innumerable fleas, and subsisting on a thrice-daily diet of native-prepared garlic and beans were just a few of the many experiences encountered by Kenneth L. Pike, today's Linguistic Institute luncheon speaker, when he began his research in the structure of Mexican Indian languages. Mr. Pike's research is now being made the basis for further study in the preparation of additional investigators to carry on similar linguistic work in Mexico and elsewhere. . . . He has spent the past three years in linguistic study for the purpose of translating the Bible for the Mixtec Indians."

Fries said in addition:

"I tried to persuade him that if you are going to make a contribution you need sound scholarship. I wanted him to be able to fit in what he was doing with what had been done. He didn't know that that was necessary. He got to work, but rather reluctantly. I felt that he became much interested in it and saw the desirability of it. It didn't take him very long — he just needed to get started.

"He had material that was excellent and was a real contribution. It was different from anything else in the field. But he didn't know **how** different, and I wanted him to know how it fitted in. I felt that this was necessary for scholarship. He did it, and he did a good job." In 1942 Pike received his Ph.D. from the University of Michigan.

Beginning in 1938, Pike along with Eugene Nida had directed the Summer Institute of Linguistics in Arkansas. He also (1942-43) collaborated as research associate in the English Language Institute at the University of Michigan, producing several volumes of material on intonation and pronunciation. His publications coupled with his directing of the Summer Institute of Linguistics, according to Dr. Fries, exerted considerable influence in "shaping" the linguistic program in the United States and abroad during that next decade.

Back in the tribe in Mexico each year, Pike continued to work on the Mixtec language and the translation of the Bible. Pike had prayed much that the translation would be more than a good piece of linguistics. He wanted the sharp edge of the Sword to penetrate hearts that needed surgery for sin.

His prayer was answered when Nalo, the faithful language helper, received Christ as Lord. It was a happy day for Pike when Nalo showed him a man-shaped outcropping of rock he had formerly worshipped. He told Pike it had been some time since he had been up to see "the old man," as he called the rock.

"You see," said Nalo, "it is only recently that my fear of him is gone."

Through Nalo's witness, others began to come to the Lord until there was a band of believers in San Miguel. Pike one day felt they were ready to sing the praises of God in their own language, so he attempted the translation of a hymn. In a tonal language this was not without its complications, as described by Pike:

"Four men, our teachers and carpenters, gathered around a folding organ, listened to the tune, giggled and balked at trying to 'fix up the words' of the rough translation I ventured from English into Mixtec. The first line I gave, then sang. They gaped, looked askance, and finally started to sing the 'Jesu . . .' by the time I reached '. . . a friend.'

" 'We don't hit it together,' they said. Several times we went over the first line. I suggested a second.

" 'No, it should be so and so,' said Nalo changing the tone (not tune; this is a tonal language à la Chinese, more or less), cutting out at the same time a syllable vital to the line length and adding a couple more to complete my rout.

" 'He delivers believers' — I departed on an excursus of my own, emphasizing His care of those who believe, since the cleavage has begun between those who study the Scriptures and those who don't. . . .

" 'Our fault it is if thus,' I managed. Nalo said that the 'thus' was no good. Lesiu suggested a 'then' to take its place. With a rare flash I found a perfect word for 'indeed' which just finished the notes of the line, a word which they deny exists if you ask them to define the indefinable thing, but which constantly occurs as oral punctuation, exclamation point, underscoring and italics all adding up to a slight 'O.K. — that's-it-of-course-believe-it-or-not-most-assuredly-man! ! '

"Over and over it we went, until beaming Nalo said, 'Oh, we're coming out at the same note now!' Then we typed it out and gave copies to three of them. After puzzling through it by word and song they decided to go home since the moon had risen to light the way.

"They know how to wait for the light, moon by night, down here. They have had to wait a long time for light on the path to heaven."

Belovéd

Alone — no longer.
Two, is one —
Meets need
    of both.

Soul longs
To tell, and ear
To hear you
    Speak!

(My commitment to writing finds some analogy in love. Love without words is straw — no building blocks for solid future. So, too, the productive scholar has not completed his task until words of essay — or song — brighten the heart and illuminate the mind.)

A SOLUTION — 1938

My commitment to writing by now headed in two directions. The interest in Bible translation — supplemented by hymns — remained as strong as ever. The need for technical linguistic writing, to serve fellow translators as well as scholars elsewhere, had by now been added.

For both of these aims to be met, however, the tone "code" hidden in the oral speech of the language had to be "cracked." We back up, from the time at which hymns could be written, to that earlier punishing struggle.

This time the story is told (in **Words Wanted**) by my sister Eunice, who was studying Mazatec on the other side of the state with her companion. She was by no means without a stake in the outcome. The two girls also had tone problems, and were waiting for the help which later they were to receive by the analytical technique developed at this time. We carry on in Eunice's words.

(Eunice has changed the names of the informants, for reasons of courtesy.)

* * *

Tone had been bothering my big brother Ken, too, as five days' journey away he worked on the Mixtec language. One day listening to the people of the village where he was staying, he'd be convinced that tone was an inherent part of the language and that it was often the only difference between words. A few days later, confused because the words frequently had different tones in a sentence from what they had when spoken alone, he would conclude that the Mixtec could not possibly be a tonal language. At one time he decided that if the same word was ever said with two different tone patterns, then that automatically proved that one was not important. With this in mind he memorized the pitch of "cloud," biko, and a number of other words. Then he set his mind to listen for those words in conversation; if he even once heard them with different pitches from those he had memorized, then, he thought, tone could be disregarded.

He didn't have long to wait. A few days later, as Ken was returning with Lucas, his informant, from a neighboring town, the man paused at the spot from which the distant mountains could be seen. He pointed in the direction of one of the biggest ones and said a sentence with "cloud" in it, and the pitch he used at that time was not the one Ken had so carefully memorized. Even as Ken responded to Lucas, he was struck by the significance of the incident. Now he **knew** that tone in Mixtec was incidental, and he rested in his decision.

But he couldn't rest long because the decision did not stand. Pairs of words continued to turn up which were different in meaning but which, except for tone, were alike in pronunciation. Once more Ken was torn with uncertainty. He wanted to grind out the answer, but he had no steady informant with whom to study. Lucas, even when he worked, came only a few hours each day, and he had worked only seven days that month.

One morning Ken watched Lucas approaching. Lucas' actions were strange, and he was too polite to be normal. Ken had guessed the reason even before they were within speaking distance. The man had come to work, but he was drunk — too drunk to be any linguistic help. Despair gripped Ken. He wanted to translate the New Testament for the Mixtec people, but how could he when he had no one to teach him the language? How could he when the tone played tricks on him? Again and again he had tried. Again and again he had failed. He wasn't even sure that tone was an essential part of the vocabulary. He thought it was, but if so, how many tones were there? Two? Three? Four? Why was it that he heard a word one way one day, and another way later? Was his ear bad, or did the tones actually change?

Discouraged, tired, conscious of failure, not only the Mixtec weighed heavily on Ken's shoulders, but the Mazatec did too. He knew that I was baffled by the Mazatec tone, and he felt that he should help his little sister. Nor was he concerned with only Mixtec and Mazatec. Otis and Mary Leal, colleagues preparing to translate for the Zapotec people, were also puzzled by things they heard. They were asking Ken questions that he couldn't answer, and he felt that if he couldn't answer them, his failure would affect not only the Mixtec work, but the Mazatec and Zapotec as well.

Ken's most immediate need was an informant — a man to take Lucas' place. He needed someone who would come every day, and who would be in condition to work after he arrived. He had tried for months to find such a person, but without success. Now the need seemed more urgent than ever.

The next day, New Year's Day, 1938, he arose before sunrise and started up the mountain that overlooked the village. Although he had had no breakfast, he carried not a lunch but a Bible. And although his need was for an informant, he was going, not to some village, but rather to a secluded nook among the pine trees. He found it, near the top of the mountain, a short distance from the footpath. Satisfied that he would not be disturbed by the occasional traveler, he knelt down on the soft, smooth pine needles. From a grateful heart he remembered and thanked the Lord for many blessings and for the help he had already received.

Then he took his Bible, and leaning against a tree he read of the Lord, whose "is the greatness, and the power, and the glory, and the victory, and the majesty," and who is "exalted as head above all." And he read that he had but to ask and that the Lord would both hear and answer. So again he got to his knees, and this time he asked for an informant, for someone who would come regularly to study. He made other petitions, and then, tired, he lay down and slept. When he awoke, he continued in prayer, and slept again when tired.

All day long without food and without water, he praised God, laid his petitions before Him, rested and prayed again. At dusk Ken came down from the mountain and went back to his hut. As he was hunting through his supplies for something to eat, Nalo, a steady, hard-working man, came in. For a little while he was quiet, watching Ken move around the room, but not for long — he soon told of his purpose for coming. He was Lucas' brother, and he knew that Ken needed an informant, and he had come to offer his services. Ken had asked him before, but he had always said that he was too busy. Now he suggested that if they studied early enough, then he could work in the cornfield afterward. Arrangements were made, and Ken went to bed rejoicing and remembering that the Lord had said, "While they are yet speaking, I will hear."

Every weekday of the month that followed found Ken and Nalo at work by 5:00 a. m. Nalo was a better informant than Lucas, and even though Nalo could be there only two hours each morning, Ken made progress. In his study he was following up a suggestion made by the eminent linguist, Sapir. One evening in 1937 during a casual conversation, Sapir had said that words of a tone language should not be analyzed one at a time, but rather that the analysis should be a matter of relationships — the pitch of each word should be compared with the pitch of the others.

In his study with Nalo, Ken was making lists of the words which were alike in pitch, and by the end of the month it was complete enough so that he felt that he could start comparing the various lists. He hoped that with the comparison he would find the answer to the tone problem that had been plaguing him. But he didn't want to take that step alone; he had already had so much trouble with Mixtec that he was afraid he would miss the answer. He wanted the help of God who created the universe. He knew that God who at Babel had scrambled the world language could bring order out of chaos and make him to understand the Mixtec system.

Once more he made his way up the mountain in order to be able to pray. He prayed for the Mixtecs, the 165,000 of them who needed to be told of Christ, and who needed His written Word. He prayed for the 55,000 Mazatecs, and the Zapotecs, and for the tribes who spoke other tone languages which he knew should and would have translators some day. He told of his need for help — how could he translate the Bible into Mixtec if he couldn't hear and record one of the essentials of that language, tone? Desperate as he was for the answer, concerned as he was for Mixtec, he asked that the solution not come to the Mixtec problem until with it he had a technique with which he could help his fellow translators. By sunset, tired, hungry, thirsty, he felt prepared for his next two-hour session with Nalo.

The next day he listened to the informant repeat the lists of previously arranged words, and he wrote down the pitch of each one as it compared with a word which he had chosen for a criterion. It was the use of the criterion word which helped him to see that the tone of speech was relative, and that the Mixtecs changed key according to their moods. By the time he had listened to the same lists several times, comparing them with different criterion words, he began to see that in some instances the tones of one word affected the tones of another. This explained why he had heard the word for "cloud" sometimes with one pitch pattern, and sometimes with another. The mysteries of Mixtec began to unfold.

One more day, that is, two more hours with the informant, and the problem with its solution which has stood the test of years was spread out before him. It was this: Each syllable of Mixtec was spoken on either a "high," "mid," or "low" pitch, and certain words exerted an influence upon other surrounding words and caused them to change from one pitch to another.

Not by Bread Alone

"Bread! give
Food!" we cry —
" 'Twill save the world!"

Will stomach's food
Suffice the soul?
Eat, and die —

Or feed on Word
By Bread from God.
Hear! — and live.

(Note: No substitute will do; but how can they hear without a preacher, **read without an alphabet?**)

Deut. 8:2; Luke 12:18-21; John 6:48-58

150

MIXTEC DIARY — 1954

I now skip over a decade. The New Testament had been translated. Our family had not been back to the San Miguel el Grande for several years — other assignments had taken my time.

One day, however, I set out on a quick trip from Puebla, to see how my friends had been getting on. By now, I had no closer friends in the world than some of these.

I wish to tell this incident myself — but in words written in the form of a letter at that time. Since I hadn't been climbing mountains for some time, I was out of shape, and had to look for a horse.

*   *   *

Puebla, Mexico
November 26, 1954

Hi Folks,

Here is a report of my trip to the Mixtec area from which I returned at 1:30 this morning.

Thursday, Nov. 18: Bus out of Puebla at 6 a. m. At noon, got off at the Desviacion. Waited till four for a bus into Tlaxiaco. A bit of rain; one wheel slipped into a ditch for an hour or so. (Crossing the rude pole bridges is sometimes a careful job. One time the helper was out watching to see if the wheels were going to touch the bridge. The chauffeur called out: "Never mind — it's okay if one tire is on the bridge" — and the other of the double wheel over air!) Arrived late — 10 p. m. — too late to find a horse for the next day.

Friday, Nov. 19: The only horse I could find was a tiny skinny thing. The hotel owner said, "Well, at least it may help" — that is, I could ride it part way and drag it the rest. I found a Trique Indian who agreed to carry my bundle — heavy because it contained six Mixtec New Testaments. But by 11 a. m. he had not shown up. It looked like rain in the mountains, and I cancelled the trip for that day and took back the horse (whom I called Rocinante, after Don Quixote), and engaged a better one for the next day, leaving time for it to be shod. It was sad losing a whole

151

day thus, when I had only four or so planned. Before supper I took a turn around the market place to see if I could find some Mixtecs from San Miguel. And what do you know — I met Ricardo walking down the road going toward San Miguel, behind his burro! Praise the Lord! He has been one of the old-timers since I was first out there, solid and true. He was on his way home from a trip, via Tlaxiaco, and had glanced into the Hotel Colon to see if any of our gang was there, but he saw no one, and being broke he kept moving out of town to get an early start for home the next morning. The Lord had timed it. Now, instead of having lost a day, it gave me a whole day on the trail with him alone, to talk over the problems in San Miguel before arrival. Things had begun to look up, he said. Nevertheless he confirmed the sad news that our chief translation helper had for some time been out of fellowship with his brethren.

Saturday, Nov. 20: We got off to a leisurely start at eight and had a comfortable trip in — ten hours or more because of the burro pace, but it left time to talk, which I prized very highly. When we stopped for rest at the 10,000-foot pass over the mountain we pulled out our Testaments (Ricardo had his small Spanish one — the Mixtec was much too big to carry on a long journey). What a joy to see it worn and used! We moved on, cheered by fellowship and conviction of the Lord's blessing. Arrived late — very dark by the time we took care of the horse. I went into town and got some tortillas and beans to eat. Went home, got out some blankets (but not enough), and passed a rather restless night. The house was in good shape, though, and seemed like home, except for an awful emptiness (my wife was in Puebla).

Sunday, Nov. 21: Up fairly early. Climbed the steep hill over the sharp valley where Angel's house can easily be seen from below. He was away, having left early for the plain, but his wife Modesta was there and was very friendly. She sent for Angel. Meanwhile, I went down to the market place, got some beans and tortillas to eat, and came back to the house. I had arranged with Ricardo to come for me to go to a section of town two hours' walk away where there were several believers, Felipe, Juan, Crecencio, Regino. Before we could get away Bernardo II had come (another old old-timer from the very beginning in 1936 in San Miguel, but not the Bernardo, now dead, for whom Stephen was given his middle name). Angel dropped in, too. From here on, things moved fast. We read from Luke 12 in the Mixtec Testaments I had there. Praise the Lord, Bernardo and Ricardo, both of whom had great trouble four years ago in reading any Mixtec, had now, since the appearance of the New Testament, learned to read quite well. How encouraging this was, after a 19-year battle! It is impossible to indicate the thrill of such a victory — they could **read!** And when they read, it was obvious they were getting the sense, since occasionally they would substitute synonyms for the words in the text — which one cannot do if he fails to understand. Later that afternoon I had Angel eat with me, but I did not try to get personal. He was under some tension, and I wanted to reestablish easy communication before doing more.

Monday, Nov. 22: ... As I stepped out of the door I saw that the horse had slipped the halter off his head and down over his neck. I went to put it back, with a bit of trepidation, because the owner had warned me not to let him loose or he might run away, since he was well fed, the prancy-dancy type, which I do not find easy to handle. As I took the halter to ease it off his face and back over his nose, he reared back so strongly I could not hold him by the neck — and he was loose. I called the school teacher Daniel to help me, but as he approached the horse trotted away, down toward the town square, in and out of the fields. As we followed I tried to get a boy to go after it, but he was even more scared than I was. Now the horse started to prance and run hard, up the mountain and out of sight. We went to the mayor and he appointed a "policia" to go after it. We then saw it, a half mile away or so, turn across the big valley and head up toward Ricardo's place. In the distance he now looked awfully tiny with the man far behind, chasing him up one canyon and down the next. Now I felt decidedly uneasy. If the horse were lost, it meant five hundred to a thousand pesos. Even if found, or if it went home, I would have lost a day or two. I tried to compose myself, deciding that perhaps it would give me another day in the Mixtec area that the Lord wanted me to use.

Tuesday, Nov. 23: About noon I had gotten my water can, locked the house, and was on the road when Angel called from across the valley that the horse was on the way back. My, was that good! It seems that he had gone up and up the mountain until dusk, and the men figured they would lose him permanently since he was heading up the mountains where he could not be caught, and was not heading home at all. By now they had been chasing the beast from twelve till six, and he still jumped all over the place. Finally they chased him until he came to a very sharp canyon cutting back in the opposite direction — and in this corner they stopped him. They could not get very near him, but Bernardo lassoed him there. So we lay around listening to the long tale — and Bernardo is as great a long-tale spinner as the Mixtec area grows.

. . . I hurried up the hill to see Angel with whom I felt I had not yet had a satisfactory talk, only good preliminaries. I met Modesta watching the cattle, and she said that Angel had gone to the town hall but had told her he would be back to come down to see me. Soon they came down, with the boys. As they came in I asked if they had eaten dinner yet — it was now getting dusky — and they said no. Nor had I, so I offered to provide the food if Modesta would help wash the dishes afterwards. All agreed, and we set to work. As we were getting the charcoal fire stirred up, in walked Lesiu with his son Pedro, and Elisabet, daughter of Preciliana, and another of the children. In the kitchen I opened up three cans of sardines I had brought for the trail, mixed them with eggs received as gifts from the people, opened up two cans of string beans and one of peas and one of Treatmeat left by the girls when they went to Mexico City. I made two huge pots of tea, lots of lemonade for the children, and used the tortillas which the neighbors had given me. While Modesta and I got that ready, Lesiu and Angel were in the other room by themselves, visiting. How precious, as a chance on neutral ground to start back together. As we sat down I asked who would say the blessing. Effie, Angel's boy, volunteered. Then Lesiu said grace for the adults. We all had a grand supper. This made a nice chitchat time, and reestablished old contacts of years before. Then I quickly brought out the Mixtec Testament so that we could read. We read from John 21. Here in our old accustomed relationships, eating around a table, we read how the Lord met His disciples and fed them breakfast. It was precious. And as the Lord did not scold, neither did we. We emphasized that the important thing was restoration without future fear. Then we prayed around. Modesta began something like this: "Oh Lord, we have all scattered like sheep. Thank you for sending Tata Ken to bring us together again." Lesiu followed, and then Angel. He prayed that he might help others in the way I had just helped him, and that he might not fear. (May God grant that request!) I believe it to be the key to power for Angel's ministry again.

The next morning I wanted to get off early — it's a long trail to Tlaxiaco. However, I was reading the Mixtec Testament when Angel knocked at the door. I had another study with him. Crecencio came and we continued. Then I stopped to get breakfast, and mop the downstairs, Angel helping me. Then Ricardo came, ready for the road, and Bernardo. Then we all stopped and prayed. Bernardo gave me money for three New Testaments plus ten pesos as a gift to help with my expenses. It so happened that I needed the cash for bus fare to get back to my family.

Golden

Years pass with love's glow
Mellowing joy.
Heaven's flame lights below
God's employ.

(Hear, again, a love poem
best reflects the joy
of looking back
through happy time.
This poem was written
for the golden wedding anniversary
of my parents-in-law.)

SAN MIGUEL: L'ENVOI — 1967

More than a decade passes once more. My wife and I were headed out to the Mixtec village after a long absence, for a final good-bye. We would tell our friends that they were on their own. Neither we — nor our colleagues who had followed us up for many years — could be expected back again.

The house, symbol of our guarantee to return, was being formally presented to the town, in a ceremony in which the governor of the state was to be represented. Linguistic and translation commitment had been met. We might never return.

This time I quote an account of the visit as I gave it to my Institute colleagues in Mexico City.

*   *   *

This trip out to San Miguel was different. I had to ask myself, "What will it be like now that we are leaving — all of us, the team?" I had left it before, but the team had not. I do not know of a spot on earth where there had been greater density of testimony, of faithful hour-by-hour and month-by-month telling of the Gospel to scores of Indians for three decades. I had watched my colleagues witness to school children passing by on their way to school, or coming in at recess. Others came to the house at all hours. Now we were leaving.

On the way to the village we went to visit the governor of the State of Oaxaca to prepare for the ceremony of presenting our home to the village of San Miguel for community use. I was impressed with the governor. He was tremendously interested in language, and in people. He was kindly and gentle, and perceptive. He was able to catch on to a mere suggestion — anything that you said about language in general or about other relationships. So that when I said of course the house itself wasn't particularly valuable he said, no, it was not the intrinsic value but the symbol which was important.

This time it was different traveling to San Miguel from Oaxaca. It took 25 flying minutes through the courtesy of the Missionary Aviation Fellowship, as over against four days on foot when I first went out. At the airstrip there was a band and a lot of people waiting for us. The school teachers had a program all lined up for presenting the house to the people. I spoke first, presenting the house. Then one of the old-time Mixtec teachers stood up and spoke in Mixtec and in Spanish. He commented especially that Pike had shown himself to be one with the town. He had carried rock on his back and had helped build a school and the town hall.

But the people of San Miguel interested me most. I found that in terms of Christian experience I would say firmly that I do not know a group of people anywhere in the world — either among my colleagues or in my church in the States — who are more firmly rooted in Christ, or more deeply committed to the Word of God. As far as I am concerned they are my equals, and in some respects they are my superiors. Intellectually, Angel is my equal. In terms of knowledge of the Scriptures, Max is my superior. Again and again as we commented on the Bible he would suggest Scripture references, and would tell me where they were to be found, chapter and verse. I would have had to use a concordance. There are two or three who know the Bible like that. One night Max came to ask me about two things in the New Testament which he couldn't understand. They were among the most obscure passages in Revelation. I asked if there were any more, and he said, no, that was all. As we talked, I would suggest related passages of Scripture, to be helpful. A couple of times he jumped ahead of me. When I had shown him the approach I was following, in each case he was quicker at finding the passages than I myself.

Among the Mixtec believers I also found counsellors in terms of certain areas of spiritual sensitivity. The day before we were to leave, Cipriano came to talk to me about another believer who had dropped having fellowship with the group of believers. He said to me, "I wonder if you have done right about this brother. Have you spoken to him about it?" I told him that this time I had decided to try a gentler approach, so I had not. Then Cipriano said, "You know, Pike, I wonder if you shouldn't speak to him — not a great deal, but 'just a little bit.' You know, the Scriptures say that we are supposed to. If we try and it doesn't work, that's all right, but I think we ought to try again — 'a little bit.' If we don't try, that's sin, too."

I was deeply moved. Here was a Mixtec believer leading **me** into the will of God. So the next day I did try. As we talked he insisted that there was no cleavage, that his failure to attend meetings was because of his town duties, and so on. I told him that the other believers did not think this.

Then I made a suggestion to him, and later to the others. Instead of trying to build up just one total church meeting as a whole, why not supplement this "particle" view of the church with a network or "field" view. Suppose that whenever an individual goes to another believer's house they should include in their visit a time of Bible study and prayer? This might bring into fellowship those who do not meet with the larger group.

My basic hypothesis was that this would develop two levels of church relationship. One of them is the formal church; the other is the network of individuals — flexible for any time or place.

As I was with the Mixtecs for this last visit, I thought much about the Scripture concerning the ninety and nine sheep, and the one that was in the mountain alone. Recently I had received a copy of an article attacking those of us involved in translating the Scriptures for such fragments. We are **wasting too much man-power** on so few, it said. While I was among the Mixtecs saying farewell, I asked myself once more, in a 30-year retrospect: Was it worth translating the New Testament for this group? My answer was an unequivocal 'Yes.' We went back to find not merely a halfway group of believers. We found strong and vigorous Christians who were our equals. They were not different from us. They were not just 'informants' or 'helpers' or 'natives,' but our equals and our superiors. They were worth the translation of the New Testament. If I am worth it, they are worth it.

The Holy Spirit brought another portion of Scripture to mind, "Where your treasure is, there will your heart be also." And I began to reflect upon my professional linguistic research and writing in relation to the investment of years among the Mixtec Indians. Just before leaving Ann Arbor for the house presentation ceremony in Mexico, I had received copies of the second edition of my major work, **Language in Relation to a Unified Theory of the Structure of Human Behavior.** As a part of the ceremony I presented a copy to the official government representative. Just before I left Michigan we had also had a little ceremony. In our Water Polo Club at the University a person who publishes a book is allowed to buy coffee for the crowd, so I begged for the honor. The chairman picked up the rather heavy volume and said, "Hmm, about three and a half pounds." Another spoke up, "Premature?" I had to reply, "Hardly — I've been working on it 17 years."

"Where is my treasure?" I asked myself. "Is it in these books?" No, I knew that my treasure was in Cipriano and Bernardo, and other Mixtec brothers who now know the Bible better than I do. It is in Cipriano who told me that I would be a sinner if I didn't speak to my erring brother again, win or lose. It is Ricardo around whom the solid core of Mixtec believers has grown. It is in my first informant Bernardo, now waiting in heaven for us, and in his widow. This, I told the Lord, is my treasure. It won't get obsolete, and it won't rust.

This is my treasure, and there is also my heart. Nor is it waste.

Waste?

Anoint His feet?
Soul-pain far
Transcends the work
Of washing sink!

Worth **that!**
A savage spear,
The scholar's heart?
Strike deep, O Word,
To "disadvantaged" soul.

Waste?!
The **"least** of these"
(Alchemy's dream!)
Transmutes to valued heart
Beyond the bravest mind —
Or Someone lies.

John 12:1-8
Matt. 25:40

Index

16-401